Michelangelo Buonarroti

Charles Clment

THE GREAT ARTISTS

MICHELAGNIOLO BUONARROTI

CALLED

MICHELANGELO

THE GREAT ARTISTS

RE-EDITED BY

HORACE SHIPP AND FLORA KENDRICK, A.R.B.S.

Michelangelo Buonarroti

BY

CHARLES CLEMENT

AUTHOR OF " MICHEL-ANGE—LEONARD DA VINCI—RAPHAEL "

logo with laurel and hand holding a brush, inscribed "S·L·M & C·Lᵈ"

LONDON

SAMPSON LOW, MARSTON & CO., LTD.

PRINTED IN GREAT BRITAIN BY PURNELL AND SONS
PAULTON (SOMERSET) AND LONDON

FOREWORD

THERE are artists whose achievement is so great that progress in the arts seems to stop with their efforts. Smaller men found schools, lead art forward, open up new avenues; great men fulfil the promise of their age and stand at the very culmination of a tendency. Imitation of their supreme performances becomes futile; yet departure from their methods seems impossible in face of their success. So Shakespeare, so Beethoven, so Michelangelo.

In sculpture, at least, Michelangelo stands so pre-eminent that the art which had begun its emancipation from mediæval crudity with thirteenth century Niccolo Pisano and climbed through the work of such men as Orcagno and Jacopo of Siena to that of Ghiberti, Donatello and Verocchio, paused for centuries at the point to which the creator of the David, the Moses and the tomb of Lorenzo carried it. Only when Rodin, almost in our own day, working as a modeller rather than as a sculptor, turned the art towards impressionism in his later work; when Mestrovitch reverted to Assyrian and Egyptian models; when the demand for expressionistic art rather than truth to nature sent some of the sculptors to primitive savage art, others to abstract form; and many to a purely decorative treatment of the facts of nature; only then did plastic art escape his domination. He remains for us still the sculptor whose works can stand alongside the best masterpieces of antiquity, and whose faithfulness alike to nature and to an ideal conception of form never falters throughout the great series of his works.

Alongside this performance as a sculptor stand his equal one as a painter and draughtsman. Indeed, the frescoes of the Sistine Chapel are for many his supreme achievement. Here his knowledge of human form and the almost infinite variety of its expressive poses, the deep under-lying humanism of the characters depicted, carried the

art of painting completely out of reach of the early
religious conventional art and yet lost nothing of its
grandeur or nobility. If Michelangelo had limitations it
was in the depicting and understanding of the female.
His female figures, both in the sculpture and in the paintings, tend to lack grace and to approximate to the ruggedness of the male. But in presenting the male, whether it
be the grace of youth or the significant boldness of age, no
artist has equalled Michelangelo.

When we turn from his art to his life we find a typical
superman of the Renaissance. A tremendous worker,
an almost savage egoist in his preoccupation with whatever
task he had set his hand to, he is the epitome of his period.
Fate and the record of his prowess brought him into
contact with two other great men, Lorenzo de Medici and
Pope Julius 2nd, and the history of their relations is the
history of Michelangelo's life. Among these giants, as
one might imagine, things were not easy; and in a temperament as difficult as the Bounarroti's his masters and patrons
found no easy protegee. The famous quarrel with Julius
forms a magnificent vignette of the life of the Renaissance.

Alongside the artistic difficulties which arose from the
conflicting desires of the princes and popes who demanded
Michelangelo's services, were those which came from the
troubled political state, and here again we find the artist
torn by conflicting loyalties. His temperamental repub-
licanism *versus* his love for the Lorenzi, his work for the
Popes and for Florence, these things could only be accepted
in a man whose every effort was so excellent that none
could afford permanently to quarrel with him if his services
could be bought by reconciliation. At one brief period
his work and an engineer and master of fortifications at
Florence made him the hero of the Republic.

Charles Clement's study holds, as it needs must, the
balance between the art and the life of the man who succeeded as sculptor, painter, poet, military engineer and
architect in the golden age of Italian art. It gives us thus
a picture of the man and his time, and most important of
all, it introduces us in turn to each of the works which have
held the world for more than four centuries in tribute to
the genius of Michelangelo.

HORACE SHIPP

CONTENTS.

———◆———

CHAPTER I.

A.D. 1475 TO A.D. 1501.

CHAPTER II.

A.D. 1501 TO A.D. 1508.

CHAPTER III.

A.D. 1508 TO A.D. 1521.

CHAPTER IV.

A.D. 1521 TO A.D. 1546.

CHAPTER V.

A.D. 1521 TO A.D. 1547.

CHAPTER VI.

A.D. 1547 TO A D. 1563.

APPENDIX.

LIST OF ILLUSTRATIONS

MICHELAGNIOLO BUONARROTI

CALLED

MICHELANGELO

MASK OF A FAUN.   BY MICHELANGELO.

(*See page* 9.)

MICHELANGELO.

THE great era of modern art, the wonderful epoch of the Renaissance, which we can in these days grasp in its entirety, differs from the older civilizations in that its development was more rapid, local, and unimpeded, and that it succeeded the gloom of the Middle Ages with hardly any period of transition. Never in the remotest times is barbarism a universal fact. It exists only among certain nations. Far as we may go back into history, we meet the civilizations of Egypt, of India, of Greece. The names of Moses, Homer, Zoroaster, Job, are intermingled with childish fables in the primitive records of mankind. The Renaissance is sudden: after ten centuries of ignorance, of barbarism, of efforts unheard-of and barren, in the dreary darkness of that sky, in the midst of all those ruins, it bursts forth into the full brightness of a summer day, almost without a dawn. Dante and Giotto open this glorious era, and with one touch give life again to Poetry and Painting. After them press the greatest men of modern times. Brunelleschi rears the dome of S. Maria del Fiore, Ghiberti casts the doors of the Baptistry, Columbus

discovers a world, Copernicus the laws of the universe: Guten-
berg renders ignorance for ever impossible: Savonarola,
Luther rouse up the individual conscience. Leonardo da
Vinci, Michelangelo and Raphael, crown this gigantic monument of human genius.

To speak of Art alone, it reaches perfection almost at one
bound. Doubtless it would be unjust to pretend that it owes
nothing to individuals, and that it came forth from nothing.
Byzantine traditions had penetrated Northern Italy, through
Venice, and in the incomparable character of the mosaics was
not without its influence upon the early Italian artists. The
Arabs, with the bright reflections of their graceful fancies, had
made a home in Sicily for beauty and for taste; the Christian painters, before they had cast off the trammels which
a jealous church had imposed upon them, had retained
some memories of the antique; the most glorious productions
of Greece and Rome came forth from the long oblivion in
which so many ages had left them, and roused the spirits of
a generation enthusiastic, eager to see, to comprehend all
things. But whatever may have been the influence of external or ancient elements upon this time, it is none the less
true that human intelligence made then a sudden movement,
and that such was the abundance and spontaneity of the new
life, that one may say humanity burst forth at the moment
from death into a fresh existence, and endowed this age with
the name which it has since retained.

Another characteristic of this period, more important, and
one which equally distinguishes it from preceding ages, is
that the works are more than ever individual, and marked
with the author's stamp. I am assuredly far from gainsaying
the personal existence of Homer, of Zoroaster, or of the name-
less sculptor of the marbles of Ægina. I can not tell whether

he who sang of the Trojan war was blind; I know not in what language or in what place men uttered the sayings of the oldest of the sages; the name of the architect of the temple to Panhellenic Zeus will probably be a mystery for ever, but these obscurities do not make me doubt that these are the works of distinct persons, of men who have lived. Still I cannot conceal from myself their collective and general character. The schools of antiquity represent the different directions of the human mind, and the successive natural modifications of sentiment. Severe teaching, the following of traditions, while clogging the flight of individual thought, carried Art to its extreme limits, by ever pushing it forward. Phidias, Scopas, Praxiteles, were less the masters of schools which bear their names, than the most illustrious representatives of the ideas which characterize them. From them flow forth both the abstract form of Grecian Art and its perfection.

Under the powerful breath of liberty regained, man recovered all the attributes of a personal existence. The superstitions, the chimeras, the terrors of the Middle Ages vanished like the recollections of the empty dreams of a troubled sleep. A brilliant light shed its rays upon a race of men, young, free, and eager. Each man went the way his taste led him; faculties the most diverse showed themselves. The character of the artist was unmistakably stamped upon his work, which as it became more living acquired a more distinct individuality, and reflected clearly his own thoughts, inclinations, and passions. Ghirlandaio, Leonardo da Vinci, Michelangelo, lived in the same city and at the same time; but who could mistake their most trifling works? Everything in this unparalleled period is grand; souls are in the fulness of inspiration. In the midst of the most difficult circumstances,

in the midst of political and social upheavings, the most violent, we rarely find these great single-minded men give way
to the demands of personal interest, disregard the dignity of
life, or forget that genius does not exempt them from the
cultivation of the humblest virtues. Not everything, it is
true, was perfect in this time, far from it; if the Renaissance
had its heroes and saints it had also its Borgias; the highest
faculties were often found associated with infamy and
cowardice. These monstrous combinations which astonish
and confound the judgment, and offend the inner sense, will
ever be seen where man is to be found; but they are com-
paratively rare, while examples of the contrary are numberless
and striking.

If there is one man who is a more striking representative of
the Renaissance than any of his contemporaries, it is Michelangelo. In him character is on a par with genius. His life
of almost a century and marvellously active, is spotless. As
an artist we can not believe that he can be surpassed. He
unites in his wondrous individuality the two master faculties,
which are, so to speak, the poles of human nature, whose
combination in the same individual creates the sovereign
greatness of the Tuscan school—invention and judgment—a
vast and fiery imagination directed by a method precise, firm,
and safe. Such giants whom antiquity would have made
into gods, are thus thrown far and wide on the pages of
history as living examples of the greatness to which our race
may attain, and to which the ambition of man may aspire.
If it is beyond our power to equal them, we can at least
contemplate them from afar, follow them, and it does not
seem to me out of place to call attention to those mighty
beings to which Liberty gave birth amidst the raging of
storms.

CHAPTER I.

BIRTH AND INFANCY OF MICHELANGELO—APPRENTICED TO
GHIRLANDAIO—LORENZO DE' MEDICI BECOMES HIS PATRON
—LIFE IN FLORENCE—GRIEF AT LORENZO'S DEATH—
STUDIES IN LITERATURE AND ANATOMY—PIERO DE' MEDICI
RECALLS HIM FROM HOME—FIRST VISIT TO ROME—THE
PIETÀ.

A.D. 1475 TO A.D. 1501.

MICHELANGELO was born on the 6th of March, 1475,
near Arezzo, in Casentino. His father, Lodovico[1]
Buonarroti Simoni, was at the time podestà of Castello di
Chiusi and Caprese. Condivi maintains, and Vasari seems to
believe, that the Buonarroti were descendants of the Counts of
Canossa, a very ancient family, closely allied by blood to
royalty. Gori, in his notes upon Condivi, even reproduces a
genealogical tree of the Buonarroti family, the original of
which, going back to 1260, he had seen. This remote origin,
however, which was ordinarily accepted in Michelangelo's
time, now appears to be more than doubtful. Still we know
this much, that the Buonarroti had been long settled in
Florence, that on several occasions they had served the Re-

---

[1] M. Clément calls him, in error, Lionardo Buonarroti.

B

public in not unimportant posts, and the name of Michelangelo requires no other nor higher origin.

His early biographers, not content with bringing him forth from a royal stem, enlarge complacently upon the omens which attended his birth. His mother, bearing him beneath her girdle, fell from a horse without serious injury. One of his brothers died in his cradle of a contagious disease without giving it to him. Lastly, at the moment of his birth, Mercury and Venus were in conjunction with Jupiter in the ascendant, a clear sign of the lofty destiny which was awaiting him.

However this may be, Lodovico Buonarroti's year of office having expired, he returned to Florence, and put the child to nurse at Settignano, where he had a small property, with the wife of a stone carver. Many years after Michelangelo used to recall this fact to Vasari. "Dear Georgio," he would say, "if my mind is worth anything I owe it to the clear air of your Arezzo country, just as it is to the milk which I sucked that I owe the use of the mallets and chisels for carving my figures."

Lodovico Buonarroti was not rich. The income of his Settignano property, which he had valued, was scarcely sufficient to provide for a numerous family. Several of his children he put into the silk and woollen business, but soon seeing that young Michelangelo had remarkable tastes, he made him begin a course of study, and sent him to Francesco da Urbino, who kept a grammar school at Florence. Here Michelangelo made no progress. The only taste he showed was for drawing, and he spent all the time he could steal from his studies in covering the walls of his father's house with sketches. His first attempts were still in existence in the middle of the eighteenth century, and Gori mentions that the Cavaliere

Buonarroti, a descendant of Michelangelo's uncle, showed him amongst other sketches, one of these, drawn in black chalk, upon a staircase wall in the Settignano Villa, representing a man with his right arm raised and his head down. The drawing was firm and vigorous, an evidence of the boy's precocity. Lodovico would not hear of an art which he thought unworthy of his family; his brothers joined him in trying to turn the bent of Michelangelo's mind. " He was often scolded " says Condivi, " and even severely beaten." He became intimate at this time with Francesco Granacci, a boy of his own age, and a pupil of Ghirlandaio, who managed to get him some of his master's drawings. Michelangelo's persistence at last overcame the prejudices of his father. He entered into an agreement with the author of the frescos in S. Maria Novella, by which the boy was to be received for three years into his workshop, and to receive a salary of twenty-four golden florins, which the master, contrary to all custom, undertook to give his pupil. The contract is dated April 1st, 1489. Michelangelo was consequently only fourteen years old.

Here in this charming church of Santa Maria Novella, which in after years he called his *fiancée*, Michelangelo was able for the first time to give himself up unreservedly to his taste for painting, under the guidance of one of the most celebrated artists of the day. So rapid was his progress that a short time after he entered the workshop Ghirlandaio remarked, " This youngster knows more than I." If we may believe Condivi too, it was not without jealousy that he saw him correcting with a firm touch his own designs and those of his best pupils.

Can we, however, as some critics have done, assign to a boy of fifteen that admirable painting in tempera, which was the greatest ornament of the Manchester Exhibition? Is the well-known precocity of Michelangelo's genius enough to account for so much knowledge and maturity? For my part I confess that I can not think so. The painting is certainly not by Domenico Ghirlandaio, as up to this time has been believed. I do not question its authenticity—that is plain. Not to speak of the size of the composition and of the drawing, of the character of the Virgin's head, of the incomparable beauty of the angels on the right, of certain tricks which Michelangelo never lost, such as making the feet too small by a refinement of elegance—giving to his children those noses, *retroussés* and somewhat faunesque, which are seen in the Sixtine, it would be evidence enough to remark the distinct relationship of this work to the Virgin of the Medici chapel. On the other hand the elegance of the draperies, an ease of drawing, which points, I confess, to recent practice in fresco, some details which recall the manner of Ghirlandaio, do not seem to me sufficient ground for assigning such a work to so young a man. What seems to me probable is, that this painting was not executed till Michelangelo had left the workshop, and had improved his taste and talent by the study of Masaccio's frescos and the Antiques in the Garden of San Marco between 1492 and 1495, during those years of early youth which must have been fruitful, yet of which the biographers have left us so little information.

Michelangelo did not finish his apprenticeship with Ghirlandaio. On the death of Ghiberti and of Donatello, Sculpture had no distinguished representative in Florence. Lorenzo de' Medici wanted to support it. He collected in his gardens by the Piazza of San Marco a large number of statues and of fragments of the antique, and he established a school of design under the direction of Bertoldo, a pupil of Donatello. He applied for pupils to the most celebrated painters in Florence. Ghirlandaio sent him Michelangelo and Granacci. Here it was that Michelangelo sculptured that *Mask of a Faun,* about which the well-known story is told, and which gained him the patronage of Lorenzo. Florence was at this time in the fulness of her splendour. To Dante, Giotto, Orcagna, had succeeded Petrarch, Brunelleschi, Donatello, Ghiberti, Masaccio. This second generation had just died out, leaving Florence full of masterpieces. Lorenzo de' Medici possessed all the qualities of a distinguished patron of art, and those also which were not likely to make his power over the citizens burdensome. Rich, generous, of good judgment, and affable, a passionate admirer of all works of genius, well-read in the old literature, and a patron of the new, surrounded by artists, poets, philosophers, scholars, himself a scholar, philosopher, and poet, he held the people, captivated as they were with the love of the beautiful, rather under his spell than under his sway.

They loved him, those Florentines; and on the eve of losing their liberty, aye, having already lost it, they did not feel the fetters with which they had submitted to be bound. Lorenzo had foreseen the genius of Ghirlandaio's pupil: he would have him in his palace, he admitted him to his table, made him the companion of his sons, allowing him five ducats a month, which Michelangelo spent in the support of his father.

Lorenzo did not stop there. He sent for Lodovico, told him that he would take charge of his son, and asked him what he could do for him himself. "Lorenzo," replied the old man, "I can do nothing but read and write, but as Marco's comrade Pucci, the douanier, is just dead, I would gladly take his place, and I think I could do the work satisfactorily." "Ah!" said the Magnificent, laughing as he gave him a slap upon his shoulder, "You will always be a poor man. However, if you would like to be Marco's comrade, you may, till something better turns up." This berth brought him in eight crowns a month, more or less, adds Condivi.

Michelangelo never left Lorenzo till his patron's death. It was, however, during those three years of calm, spent in intercourse with the most learned men of the time, Poliziano, Pico della Mirandola, and the Platonist, Marsilio Ficino, that his mind developed, matured and acquired its breadth and accuracy. Poliziano admitted him to special intimacy. By his advice he produced the bas-relief of the *Battle of Hercules with the Centaurs*, and the graceful *Madonna*, works, in which, according to Vasari, he tried to imitate Donatello. He spent several months in copying Masaccio's frescos in the church del Carmine. About the same time too he studied anatomy at the hospital of Santo-Spirito, and made a *crucifix* in wood for the prior, who had procured his admission. He continued his studies of the Antique in the gardens of San Marco, of which Lorenzo had given him a key. So great was his progress that it often excited the jealousy of his companions. It was this that brought upon him the blow from Torriggiano's fist, which broke his nose, and helped to give that well-known rugged and almost savage expression to his features, which even before this were strongly marked.

Lorenzo died in 1492. In him Michelangelo lost more than a patron. "So great," Condivi tells us, "was his grief at the death of his friend, that he remained for several days unable to do anything." In the long course of his life we shall see more than once what a tender and loving recollection he retained of this name of Medici, and in what dilemmas he was placed by his gratitude and his republican feelings. Under such circumstances it is doubtless a man's part either to surrender his individuality or to take an independent course without regard to the feelings of his heart. It is not easy to keep the mean between ingratitude and servility. As regards this, never even in the midst of perils was Michelangelo found wanting; he was neither ungrateful nor servile, and this grand trait in his character is no less noteworthy than his genius.

On his return to his father's house Michelangelo made a *Hercules* in marble, seven feet eight inches in height, which later on was bought with other works of art by Giovanni Pattista della Palla for Francis the First, and sent to France. It is not known what became of it. Piero de' Medici, the unworthy son of Lorenzo, induced Michelangelo to come back to his rooms in the palace ; he often consulted him about the purchase of gems and antiques. Piero no doubt was in his way alive to the merits of his guest, for he occupied him in making snow statues, and boasted of having in his house two rare men, Michelangelo and a Spanish valet, who in addition to his marvellous beauty was so swift of foot that a horse at full speed could not outstrip him.

Piero de' Medici, with all his external advantages, was wanting in the discretion, address, the affability and kindly feeling, which had established the fortunes of his father and made him actual master of Florence. His arrogance became more unbearable every day. The popular party awoke and Savonarola held out his hand to Charles the Eighth. The fall of Piero was imminent. Michelangelo, unwilling either to oppose or to support him in a struggle against personal friends, or to preserve a neutrality which his friendship with

Lorenzo and his relations with Piero would have rendered suspicious, left Florence and betook himself to Venice. Finding nothing to do there he went to Bologna, where by a lucky accident he became acquainted with Aldovrandi, one of the Council of Sixteen, who got him several commissions. Aldovrandi kept Michelangelo with him for more than a year, loading him with tokens of his friendship and esteem, and "charmed with his beautiful pronunciation, making him read Dante, Petrarch, Boccaccio, and other Tuscan poets to him."

On his return to Florence in 1495, Michelangelo made a statuette of *St. John*, and also the famous *Sleeping Cupid*, which was the cause of his first visit to Rome. Biographers have insisted on a somewhat childish story about this statue. If I tell it in a few words, it is because of the lasting effect that Michelangelo's stay in the Eternal City had upon the rest of his life. Lorenzo, son of Piero de' Medici, saw this figure and thought it so beautiful that he advised Michelangelo to bury it, so as to give it the appearance of age, and then to send it to Rome, where it would be sure to pass for an antique, and where he would get a much better price for it than in Florence. The Cardinal San Giorgio was taken in by the device and bought the statue.

When he learned that he was the victim of a fraud, he sent one of his gentlemen to discover the author of it, and furious at the idea of being cheated he broke off the bargain and recovered his money. Such is Vasari's tale. He does not, however, seem to think that Michelangelo was a party to the trick. He adds that, despite his anger, the Cardinal brought Michelangelo to Rome, though he left him, it is true, for a year without employment. A very curious letter, of which only a few fragments exist, written by Michel angelo to this Lorenzo de' Medici, directly he got to Rome, completes and corrects the story as told by his biographer. It shows too, that from his early youth Michelangelo was animated by that scrupulous integrity which remained the rule of his life. Nothing less than the stir which this affair made would induce us to believe that at the end of the 15th century and in Rome any one could have taken a statue of the youthful Florentine master for an antique. Vasari tells us, it is true, that the Cardinal had no taste for art whatever, and that he was a very ignorant man.

Michelangelo lived in Rome from 1496 to 1501. How were these five years occupied? This is just what we do not perfectly know. He was already famous, in all the vigour of youth, and we can hardly suppose that the four statues now in existence which date from this time were the only works which occupied him there. For, not to mention the fifteen figures for the library of Siena Cathedral, which were ordered by Cardinal Piccolomini, of which we have but very inadequate information, though four of them seem to have been completed, we only know of the *Bacchus*, the *Cupid* of the South Kensington Museum, the *Adonis* of the Uffizi at Florence, and the *Pietà* now at St. Peter's, which belong to this first stay in Rome. The *Bacchus* was ordered by an amateur, named Jacopo Galli : the *Pietà* by Cardinal Jean de la Grolaye de Villiers, Abbot of St. Denis, Ambassador of Charles VIII. to Alexander VI., and not by Cardinal Amboise, as Condivi and Vasari think. As to the *Adonis* of the Uffizi at Florence, it is probably the statue which Michelangelo began directly he got to Rome, and of which he speaks in his letter to Lorenzo de' Medici.

The *Pietà* of St. Peter's reveals the course which Michelangelo was going to take more distinctly than any of his early works. The marble shall no longer represent the beauty of form in an abstract and general manner; it shall translate, under the touch of a mighty hand, the thoughts and feelings of the artist's soul. "The greatest artist may not shut up his conceptions in the heart of the marble; he needs a hand obedient to the thought to make the block give it forth. An obedient hand will ever try to give the stone a voice it has never had before." This Virgin possesses the youthful yet grave beauty which is peculiar to Michelangelo's women. The form of the Christ stretched out upon his mother's knees, even in the repose of death, bears marks of the sufferings which the God-man has just passed through. The undeniable beauty of the legs, the joints, the extremities, is a foreshadowing of the most perfect and characteristic works of the master.

The production of this *Pietà* was a great event in Rome, still we know that its strongly-marked expressions, its "speaking forms" created some astonishment. Vasari is satisfied with treating as "fools" those who maintained that Michelangelo had given the Virgin too youthful an appearance, for the true age which he had allowed the Christ.

Condivi, with less brevity and contempt, has given us the explanation which he had from Michelangelo himself. "Don't you know," he said, "that chaste women keep their youthful looks much longer than others? Isn't this much more true in the case of a Virgin who had never known a wanton desire to leave its shade upon her beauty! . . . It is quite the contrary with the form of the 'Son of God,' because I wanted to show that he really took upon him human flesh, and that he bore all the miseries of man, yet without sin."

Whatever be the value of Michaelangelo's explanation,

the individuality which is the dominant feature of his genius, and which shows itself in intended and deliberate expressions, is already plainly manifest in these early works. Hereafter it is destined to become still more marked and to be the covering of that powerful, lofty, original form which makes the slightest works of Buonarroti immortal creations. Michelangelo will increase in greatness and surpass every one who has gone before him; his giant imagination will hurl forth upon the world new forms truer than life. Intoxicated with his own genius, he will climb the loftiest summits of art; he will go to the utmost limits of rash daring, even into excesses; but, from his first steps, it is a giant who is striding onward, and if at the end of his long course he has preserved the fervour and activity of youth, he has never known the uncertainty, the feebleness, the groping after a road, which generally make the setting out into life so bewildering.

CHAPTER II.

THE DAVID—MARSHAL GIÉ—" POTS-DE-VIN "—ROBERTET—
LEONARDO DA VINCI—THE CLIMBERS—POPE JULIUS
II. AND HIS TOMB—BUONARROTI'S RAGE, FLIGHT AND
SUBMISSION AT BOLOGNA—COLOSSAL STATUE OF THE
POPE.

A.D. 1501 TO A.D. 1508.

AFTER the expulsion of the Medici, Florence was for some years the scene of incessant conflicts. The death of Savonarola, which secured the defeat of the violent reformers, brought the moderate party into power, and men began again with more eagerness than ever to cultivate the arts, which had been for a moment proscribed by the fiery Dominican. Michelangelo longed to see his native place again, and soon found the opportunity to return. At the works of Santa Maria del Fiore there had been for a long time an enormous block of Carrara marble, which several sculptors had tried in vain to make use of, but had only succeeded in spoiling. Soderini had urged Leonardo da Vinci to take it in hand, but he had declared that he could do nothing with it. Some friends wrote to Michelangelo. He wanted no temptation to undertake an impossibility; he

was on the spot at once, and guaranteed a figure from it
without any patching. He obtained a concession of the
block to him by a resolution of the 16th of August, 1501,
and was to produce from it a statue of *David*, which he was
to finish in two years ; he was receive six gold florins per
month in payment. He built a workshop on the spot, and
shut himself up for eighteen months without letting any one
see his work. The colossal figure in front of the palace of
the Signory was the result of this solitary toil. In the
execution of this statue Michelangelo was no doubt
hampered by the dimensions of the marble. He was obliged
to abandon an idea which he had at first of giving more
movement to the figure. A design of the utmost interest,
formerly in the possession of Mariette and described by him,
which after many wanderings has come back to the Louvre,
reveals the first conception of this work. David is planting
his foot upon the head of Goliath. This action, which
brought the knee forward, made the execution of the figure,
according to this conception, impossible, because of the form
of the marble. Michelangelo had to give up his first intention, and we are compelled to admire in this statue rather
the dignity of the attitude, the graceful power of the figure,
the consummate skill and finish of the work, than the exact
representation of an historical personage. Contemporaries
were evidently struck with the undecided character of this
figure, for Condivi calls it simply " The Giant."

The *David* was put in its place on the 8th of June, 1504,
and completely finished on the 8th of September, in the same
year. The place which this colossal figure was to occupy was
agreed upon finally after stormy disputes. The difficult task
of transport was accomplished under the direction of Polla-
juolo and San Gallo. Documents preserved among the

archives of Santa Maria testify to the intelligence and anxiety which the Florentines display in art administration. The names of members of the commission to investigate everything in connexion with the *David* are preserved. They are those of the most eminent artists of the day: Leonardo da Vinci, Perugino, Filippino Lippi, Ghirlandaio. There is no trace of interference by incompetent authority,—opinions were divided; some wanted to set up the David under the Loggia dei Lanzi, others in its present position,[1] on the left of the entrance gate of the Palace of the Signory. Michelangelo was summoned on the proposal of Lippi to give his opinion, being the man who had made the statue. The Gonfaloniere Soderini came to see him at work touching up some parts, and took it into his head to criticize the nose of the David. It was too large. The artist made cruel jest of him. He mounted the scaffolding, taking up with him a handful of marble dust, which he sprinkled over his critic, while he all the while pretended to be altering the nose with his chisel. Then he came back to the Gonfaloniere. "Well, what do you think of it now?" "Admirable!" replied Soderini; "you have given it life." Michelangelo came down laughing at the magistrate, "like so many other clever connoisseurs, who speak without knowing what they are talking about."

While he was employed on the *David* in marble, in 1502, Soderini commissioned Michelangelo, on behalf of the State of Florence to execute another statue of *David*, but in bronze, which was to be sent to Marshal de Gié. This, in the course of events, was handed over to the treasurer, Robertet, in 1508. If it be not destroyed, it should be still in France, but

---

[1] The "David" is now under a glass roof in one of the courts of the "Academy of the Fine Arts."

no one knows absolutely what has become of it. It would be therefore useless to speak of it, if it had not been the cause of much anxiety to Michelangelo, and if the documents preserved in the archives of Florence did not give us some curious accounts of the relations which existed at that time between the Florentine Republic and France. We gather from these documents that proceedings, which we vulgarly call *pots-de-vin*, were employed at that time, and in a way which would, no doubt, seem very childish now-a-days! Pierre de Rohan, Marshal de Gié, was not only the important political personage whom we know. After having served Louis XI. and Charles VIII. in war and government, he had preserved the favour of Louis XII., and during his Italian campaigns at the head of the French armies, his taste for art had developed. He willingly supported the Florentine ambassadors in their difficulties with France, and already, in 1499, the Signory of Florence has recognized his services by sending him twelve busts, which had probably served to adorn his house, " the Grove." During one of his visits to Florence, the Marshal had noticed Donatello's statue of *David*, now in the Uffizi. He wanted one like it, and the ambassadors from Florence wrote the following letter upon the point to the government of the Republic.

"Marshal de Gié seems well disposed towards our city, and earnestly entreats us to inform your lordships how glad he would be if you would have a bronze statue of *David* cast for him, like the one which he has seen in the palace court. He says that he will pay all expenses ; but we are sure that at the bottom of his heart he is reckoning upon its being given to him as a present."

The magistrates seem to accede to the marshal's wishes readily. "We have tried," they write, "to find a man who can execute a statue of *David* like the one which you want for Marshal de Gié, but there is a dearth of good masters. However, we will not fail to do our utmost." The Marshal is impatient, he begs the ambassadors to remind their lordships that he is most anxious to have this statue. The latter add " that he is so well disposed, that he is deserving of much more." Its execution is entrusted to Michelangelo, and by the end of 1502 it is already far advanced.

The Gonfaloniere writes again to the embassy that it is being pushed on as fast as possible ; " but in the matter of painting and sculpture, it is impossible to make definite promises ;" that it will be ready by Midsummer, if Michelangelo keeps his promise, " upon which it won't do to reckon too confidently, remembering the flightiness of those sort of people." It is certain that after setting himself with the greatest earnestness to this figure, Michelangelo seems to have neglected it for the cartoon of the *Battle of Pisa* and for the twelve statues which had been ordered for Santa Maria, and he deserves the hard words which his friend Soderini did not spare. At last, the Marshal having offended Queen Anne, fell into disgrace, and thus Michelangelo got some respite.

The correspondence is, however, resumed in 1505, upon the following occasion. The Republic of Florence owed France a somewhat considerable sum of money, of which the treasurer, Robertet, demanded immediate payment. The ambassador Pandolfini at first endeavoured to treat directly with the King, but he soon perceived that it was necessary to have recourse to some intermediate person. " The King," says he, " will take no trouble, he allows himself to be governed entirely by others, and with four words uttered at the right moment he is made to do what they want. He said this very morning, ' The Florentines must be made to pay the money

Michelangelo
From the portrait in the Uffizi

Face page 20

The Head of Adam   [Sistine Chapel

Face page 21

they owe at any cost.' Matters are urgent; the ambassador is
put into communication with some one about the treasurer.
The latter speaks to his master, who flies into a passion,
declaring that the Florentines are ungrateful, that all this
comes of the Gonfaloniere's avarice; that his services have
been better rewarded under other circumstances; that he received the ring which he wears upon his finger after the
revolution of Arezzo, and a silver bowl in the time of Nicolo.
"See," he adds, "what good friends these people are; they
made a statue for Marshal de Gié, and when he fell into
disgrace, they kept it back." The agent concludes by assur-
ing them that if some hundreds of crowns were given every
year to Robertet, they would derive a wonderful benefit from
it. "*Tanto fructo che maraviglieresti.*" Robertet finished
by making it understood that if the statue were sent to him
everything would be easily arranged, and in fact, from that
moment the best relations seem to exist between the ambassadors and the severe treasurer of Louis XII. The *David* is
cast, but requires corrections. Michelangelo is in Rome,
employed in painting the vault of the Sixtine; the Pope
will not grant him leave of absence, not even for twenty-five
days, and there is no one in Italy, writes Soderini, who is
able to finish a work of such importance. He and he only
must direct the work, for any one else ignorant of his conception might spoil it. They were obliged, however, to
abandon the idea of having the statue finished by Michelangelo, and we see by a letter of Soderini of October the
14th, 1508, that he had employed another artist to repair it.
The *David* is embarked at Leghorn at the end of 1508.
Robertet is delighted with it, he wants to place it in the
court of his palace at Blois, but wants a column for a pedestal.
This was too much for Soderini, he refused point-blank. I

c

have already said that this statue has disappeared, it has probably been melted down, whence we may conclude that "no good comes of ill-gotten gains."

To return to Michelangelo. He was engaged by a contract, dated 25th April, 1503, to finish in twelve years the twelve statues, eight feet high, for Santa Maria del Fiore, which I have already mentioned. He only hewed roughly out one of them, that of *St. Matthew*, now in the Florence Academy. It is not known why he abandoned this work. His fellow-citizens thought so much of it that they arranged that the house which was built expressly for these works should gradually become his own property as he delivered these statues. He worked at the same time on two circular bas-reliefs, representing the *Virgin and Child*, the one for Taddeo Taddei, the other for Bartolommeo Pitti. One of these works may be seen in the Uffizi Gallery; the other, which, although unfinished, is one of his most wonderful works, is in London, in one of the rooms of the Royal Academy. Vasari mentions another bas-relief in bronze which was sent into Flanders, but is now unknown.

It was between 1502 and 1504 and "not to give up painting altogether," that Michelangelo painted in tempera the celebrated *Virgin of the Tribune* in Florence. Of all the easel-pieces attributed to Michelangelo, this is the only one whose authenticity has never been doubted. The *Parcæ* in the Pitti palace, which have for a long time passed as the work of his hand, and the inspiration, arrangement, and design of which certainly belong to him, are now attributed with probability to Rosso, the Florentine. The *Virgin of the Tribune* has been often engraved; everybody knows it, and I will not describe it. The expression is hard and harsh, and despite qualities of the first order, it is not an attractive picture. Michelangelo was not at his ease in too restricted a space; he wanted room in which to give full scope to the daring flights of his imagination. As a painter he was destined to show his power only upon the vaults of the Sixtine, and I think that he would readily have said of all easel-work that which is attributed to him about oil paintings; "that it was only fit for women." He has been severely reproached for having helped to make the religious character of this painting unnatural, by putting in nude figures in the background. It is undeniable that at that time he broke through the traditions of ecclesiastical Art of the Middle Ages, and of the early days of the Renaissance, and that he was in his after course to make the breach still wider. It is to be remarked moreover, that before him Luca Signorelli had done just as much, as may be seen in his *Madonna* in the Uffizi Gallery. and still more plainly in his wonderful frescos in the cathedral of Orvieto.

In the spring of 1503, the magistrates of Florence resolved to have the Council Hall of the Signory ornamented with paintings, and commissioned Leonardo da Vinci, then at the height of his fame, to undertake one of the sides. Leonardo was already at his work, when Michelangelo was in his turn commissioned to paint the opposite wall. There would not have been, as is generally believed, a sort of competition in which the author of the *Last Supper* at Milan, far advanced in years would have been beaten by his young rival. These paintings were not executed. Leonardo, after getting on some way with his, was disgusted, and threw it up. The cartoon which he had prepared has not come down to us. There only remains for us, to form an idea of the composition, a fragment engraved by Edelinck after a copy by Rubens, but we try in vain to recognize the work of the Florentine master through the interpretation of the Flemish painter. Leonardo had chosen for the subject of his composition an episode in the *Battle of Anghiari*, which is finished by the defeat of the Milanese General Piccenino. The fragment, not at all satisfactorily engraved by Edelinck, represents some horsemen disputing the possession of a standard; probably it formed only an inferior part of a vast whole, and we are compelled to deplore the loss of one of the most important works of Leonardo. The cartoon which Michelangelo had prepared was no better preserved, and perished during the troubles of 1512. Vasari accuses the jealous Bandinelli of this act of sacrilegious destruction. Some fragments of it were preserved at Mantua up to 1595, but even these fragments have disappeared. The loss of this cartoon is certainly irreparable, happily it is not complete. In the 16th century Marc' Antonio and Agostino Veneziano engraved some of the figures of it, well-known under the name of *The Climbers*, probably after drawings by Raphael, who studied this great work during his stay in Florence from 1506 to 1508.

The most celebrated painters vied with each other in copying it, and San Gallo, according to Vasari, reproduced it in chiaroscuro. This must be that painting in black and white, which after having been for a long time in the hands of the Barberini family, must have found its way into England; it is now at Holkham Hall, and has been well engraved by Schiavonetti.

Michelangelo began this cartoon in October, 1504, and the valuable documents published by Doctor Gaye inform us that he worked upon it in February, 1505, consequently a very little while before his second departure from Rome. He perhaps worked at it again during his stay in Florence, on his way to Carrara in search of marble for the tomb of

Julius II., or even on his return, and we see that in the month of August, 1505, he had completely finished his work. Eight or ten months therefore had sufficed to bring him to the end of this grand undertaking. True it is that he shut himself up, as usual, in his workshop at San Onofrio, and would let nobody see his work before it was finished. He chose for the subject of his composition an episode in the war with Pisa. Some Florentine soldiers bathing in the Arno are surprised by the enemy's horse. The trumpets are sounding the alarm, some of the soldiers are jumping out of the water, and helping each other out, others are throwing on their clothes in haste or seizing their arms. This scene of confusion is more suitable than any other could have been for exhibiting to perfection those remarkable and original qualities, that knowledge of anatomy, that daring in composition, and boldness of drawing which so eminently distinguish the young Florentine master. Although Luca Signorelli had already introduced in his Orvietan frescos nude figures of great importance, no painter had as yet approached the human form with that boldness and freedom, or triumphed with such ease over almost insuperable diffities. So, when in 1506 this cartoon was exhibited for the first time in the saloon of the Popes, adjoining Santa-Maria-Nuova, it excited a surprise to which all contemporaries bear witness. Benvenuto Cellini maintains that Michelangelo never received so lofty an inspiration, not even in the Sixtine paintings; and adds that this composition with that of Leonardo are worthy of being "the school of the world."

Whatever may have been the influence of the Cartoon of the *Battle of Pisa* upon contemporary artists, who studied it as the most important existing work of the greatest genius of the time, it is necessary to be on one's guard against a blind belief in the enthusiastic biographer, who wrote the early part of the life of Michelangelo upon very inaccurate and incomplete authorities, and who asserts among other things that Raphael, when at Siena with Pinturicchio, came to Florence in 1502 to study Michelangelo's work. The cartoon was not begun in 1502. There is, moreover, abundant proof that Raphael did not come to Florence for the first time till 1504, and as Michelangelo's work was not exhibited till 1506, it was not until then that Sanzio could have derived any benefit from it. The influence of Buonarroti upon Raphael is, however, undoubted, and Vasari is only wrong in the matter of the time when the latter began to subject himself to it. The effect produced upon the painter of the *Sibyls* of the Pace by the author of the Sixtine was so perfectly admitted by contemporaries, that Julius II. said to Sebastiano del Piombo : "Look at Raphael's works : he gave up Perugino's style as soon as ever he saw what Michelangelo had done, and followed him as closely as possible." He added : "He is a terrible man, no one can live side by side with him."

If one may believe Vasari, it was in 1503, immediately after his elevation to the Pontificate, that Julius II. determined to have a tomb made for himself, summoned Michelangelo to Rome, and bade him design a monument which should throw into the shade everything that had been seen up to that time ; now we know that Michelangelo was still in Florence in the February of 1505, and could not have set out for Rome till about that time, that is to say, two years later than his biographer assigns. He probably set to work at once upon the design for the tomb, which Julius accepted with his usual enthusiasm, and ordered to be executed at once. Then he went to Carrara, where, by his own account he lived for eight months. During his stay in that city he was only able to finish four statues and to block out eight others, as Vasari asserts. He was not, however, indolent. It is evident from the contract with the bargemen, who were to bring his marbles to Rome, that he had blocked-out two figures there; but this takes us far away from Vasari's account. The marbles arrived; half the space about St. Peter's was covered with them. Julius busied himself about this tomb with the restless activity which he displayed in everything. He had a covered bridge made leading from his palace into Michelangelo's workshop, "where he often went to look for him to talk about his burial and other things, as he would have done with a brother." How was it that this intimacy suddenly changed to such a coldness that Michelangelo resolved to give up the works which he had undertaken with so much zeal, and to fly from Rome? The reasons alleged by his biographer to explain the origin of the quarrel are evidently inadmissible. Vasari asserts, among other things, that the Pope got over Michelangelo's workmen and secretly went into the Sixtine to see the vault paintings, and that Michelangelo seeing him, hid himself upon the scaffolding and threw some dust down upon the Pontiff which almost smothered him. However, it could not have been even a question of the Sixtine paintings at that time, for they were not commenced till 1508. Everything leads to the belief that the friendship of this terrible patron was a nuisance to Michelangelo, as it intruded upon his customary solitude in work; that with the intractable disposition which we all know he had, and Julius becoming, at least for the moment, indifferent about the tomb, the sculptor did not conceal his chagrin from the Pope, and from it proceeded a coldness which between two persons of their temper could only finish with an outbreak. Vasari relates the catastrophe of this drama :—

" Whilst Michelangelo employed himself in these works, a last cargo of marble from Carrara arrived at Ripa, and was drawn to the open space near St. Peter's. As the bargemen had to be payed, Michelangelo, as usual, went to the Pope to ask for money. That day His Holiness was engrossed in Bologna affairs. Our artist settled the accounts out of his own pocket, thinking that he would soon be repaid. Some time after he went back to the palace to speak to the Pope about it, but he found the same difficulty in obtaining admission, and a servant told him not to distress himself, for he had received orders not to admit him. ' But,' says a Bishop who was there at the time, ' don't you know the person whom you are refusing ?' ' Yes, I know him very well ; but I am here to execute the orders of His Holiness,' replied the servant. Michelangelo, indignant at such treatment, for till that time all doors had been open to him, said to the footman : ' When the Pope wants me, you can tell him that I have gone elsewhere.' He returned home at two o'clock in the night, gave orders to two of his servants to sell all his goods to the Jews and to join him in Florence. He mounted his horse, and did not stop till he got to Poggibonzi in Florentine territory. He had scarcely reached the place, when he was overtaken by five couriers, one after another, bearing the most urgent letters from His Holiness, enjoining upon him to return to Rome, under pain of incurring his displeasure. Invitations and threats were alike unavailing. All the couriers could get from him by supplication was a line to the Pope, begging him henceforth to excuse his absence, but " having been treated like a beggar in return for his services and his attachment, His Holiness might choose some other sculptor."

Julius did not expect resistance, and was extremely violent. He wrote three briefs to the Signory of Florence to demand the return of the fugitive; but Michelangelo was by no means anxious to expose himself to his resentment. Rather than return to the Pope he resolved to leave his native country and to accept the invitation of the Sultan, who wanted him to build a bridge to unite Pera with Constantinople. Julius threatened; Soderini parleyed, wishing to secure the safety of his fellow-citizen and friend, and not caring, on the other hand, to irritate his powerful neighbour beyond measure. Michelangelo would listen to nothing. "He is so frightened," writes the Gonfaloniere, "that notwithstanding the brief of his Holiness, he will have the Cardinal of Pavia send us a letter under his own hand promising us perfect security and impunity. We have done and will do our utmost to make him return; but we assure you that if gentle means are not adopted, he will leave this, as he has twice already made up his mind to do." He wrote, moreover, to the Cardinal da Volterra: "We have seen Michelangelo, and have done our utmost to persuade him to return; but he is still mistrustful, because your Lordship makes no definite promise." Soderini was saying at the same time to Michelanglo, "You have tried an experiment which the King of France would not have ventured. The time is past for entreaty. We will not expose the state to a war with the Pope on your account. Therefore make ready and be gone." In the midst of these discussions, Julius II. had entered Bologna, but the events of the war had not made him forget his sculptor. In fact, it was from that city that the Cardinal da Volterra wrote on the part of Julius to the Signory of Florence one of the most urgent letters, which at last decided Michelangelo. He set out for Bologna about the 1st of December, and it is worth while to see the warmth and tenderness with which the excellent Gonfaloniere commends him to the Cardinals of Pavia and Volterra :—" The bearer of these presents is Michelangelo the sculptor, whom we send to you to be at the disposal of his Holiness. We certify to your Lordship that he is a young man of mark, and in his profession stands alone in Italy, perhaps even in the whole world. We cannot too earnestly commend him to you. He is of such a mould that you may get from him all you want by kind words and actions. Only show him kindness and friendship, and he will do such things as will make all who see them marvel." The whole character of Michelangelo is set forth in these few lines of his friend. Prompt, hasty, unyielding, suspicious of intrigue, business, tumult, and everything which took him from his art and tore him from his solitude, he was easy to lead, as strong men always are, with a little show of consideration and affection. Plunging into the midst of difficulties with eagerness, or when he saw some duty to be fulfilled, he was as ready to withdraw when his feeling cooled or when he considered himself at liberty. Upon this point the judgment of Condivi is in accord with that of the Gonfaloniere. " As often happens," he says, " to those who give themselves up to the contemplative life, he was timid, except when he had a subject for just indignation, and when wrong or injustice fell upon himself or others. Then he had more courage than those who are held to be courageous. Under ordinary circumstances he was very patient."

Condivi has given us a lively account of the first interview between Michelangelo and Julius after this quarrel, and one which gives us a good idea both of the characters and the times :—" Michelangelo arrived at Bologna in the morning, and went to hear mass at San Petronio. There he met some

of the Pope's grooms, who recognized him, and carried him to
his Holiness. The Pope was at table in the Palace of the
Sixteen. When he saw him, he said, with an indignant
expression, ' You seem to have expected that we were going
to look for you instead of you coming to us.' Michelangelo
bent his knee, and raising his voice excused himself, explain-
ing that he had acted with no malice, but from indignation,
and that he could not endure being driven away as he had
been. The Pope kept his head down without any reply, and
seemed much troubled. Then a Bishop, who was charged by
Soderini to excuse Michelangelo and to present him, inter-
posed, saying, ' Pardon him, your Holiness. He has sinned
in ignorance. These painters are all like this.' The Pope
answered hotly: 'You fool to find fault, when I don't!
You're an ass, to insult this man! Out of my sight; to
the devil with you!' And as the Bishop did not move, he
was put out by the domestics, with a shower of blows into
the bargain. The Pope having discharged most of his anger
upon the head of the Bishop, bade Michelangelo approach,
gave him his pardon and benediction, and told him not to
leave Bologna without his orders. A short time afterwards,
he sent for him and ordered a statue of himself for the front
of San Petronio. Michelangelo finished this, which was
more than three times the size of life, in sixteen months. The
Pope came to see the model of it before leaving Bologna, and
the sculptor, at a loss what to put in the left hand, asked him
if he would like a book. "What!" replied Julius, "a book?
—a sword! I am no book-worm; not I." Then he joked
upon the bold movement of the right arm, and said smiling,
"Is it a blessing or a curse which your statue is giving?"
"Holy Father, it is threatening the people in case they are not
good." This statue, for which Michelangelo received 1000

golden ducats from the Commune of Bologna, was placed over the grand entrance of San Petronio on the 21st Feb. 1508. It remained there till 1511, the time when the Bentivoglios came into Bologna, and the people broke it in a fury. The Duke Alfonso of Ferrara bought the pieces, and had them made into a piece of artillery which he called the "Julienne." The loss of the figure of this terrible *Julius II.* by Michelangelo is the more unfortunate, as this statue has left fewer traces than other works of the Florentine sculptor which have likewise perished. The head, however, had been spared; it weighed six hundred pounds, and the Duke Alfonso, who preserved it in his own room, used to say that he would not take its weight in gold for it. But it is not known what has become of it; it has probably perished like the rest.

CHAPTER III.

RETURN TO ROME—TOMB OF JULIUS II.—SAN LORENZO—
PAUL III.—THE "MOSES"—THE "CAPTIVES"—WORK IN
THE SIXTINE—DIFFICULTIES—GENIUS AND STYLE—LEO X.
—SERRAVEZZA MARBLE QUARRIES.

A.D. 1508—A.D. 1521.

IN 1508 Michelangelo returned to Rome and resumed his
work on the tomb, which had been interrupted by his
quarrel with Julius and his flight from Rome. He was soon
to give it up a second time. Bramante had persuaded the
Pope that it was unlucky to build his own sepulchre. He
advised him to employ Michelangelo in painting the chapel,
which his uncle Sixtus IV. had built. So at the beginning
of this year he put the first touch to that giant work of decoration which was destined to be his grandest achievement.
We shall see how stoutly he resisted the importunity of
Julius, yet with what ardour he entered into that stupendous
undertaking, and with what rapidity he completed it, when
once he had made up his mind to give way. First, however,
since at the period to which we have come, most of the
statues were blocked out or finished which now adorn the

tomb of Julius II. at San Pietro in Vincoli, and those still
more numerous which formed part of the original design and
which have been dispersed, I should like to give a general
idea of this monument, so as not to come back to it again. I
wish also to show through what a series of modifications the
original design passed, and what troubles it brought upon the
author. Vasari and Condivi do not quite agree in their
description of the design for this monument, as it was conceived by Michelangelo and adopted by Julius II. I shall
follow Condivi's account, which pretty well agrees with a
drawing of it from Michelangelo's own hand, in the possession of Mariette, described by him, and at this moment
forming part of the Florence collection. The tomb was
to be isolated. On each of its faces were to be four
slaves standing, chained to terminal columns, which supported the cornice, and in niches between these groups two
figures of Victory trampling upon prostrate prisoners. Above
the cornice which surmounted these decorations were to be
eight sitting figures, two on each face, representing the
Prophets and the Virtues. The *Moses* was to be one of these
statues. The sarcophagus placed between them was surmounted by a pyramid, having at the apex an angel holding
a globe. Vasari adds that there were to be in all more than
forty figures without reckoning the children and other ornaments. According to him the cornice was only to support
four figures : Active, and Contemplative Life, St. Paul and
Moses. The sarcophagus was to be supported by two figures,
which Condivi does not mention : Heaven, seeming to rejoice
that the soul of Julius had gone to inhabit the eternal glory,
and Earth weeping over the loss of the Pontiff. This ambitious design was not altered till 1513 ; but after the death of
Julius, Cardinals Santiquatro and Aginense, and the Duke of

Urbino, his executors, reduced to six the number of statues which were to contribute to the decoration of the monument, and to 6,000 ducats the sum of 10,000, which was to have been expended on it.

From 1513 to 1521 Leo X. who was less concerned in finishing the tomb of his predecessor than in endowing his native city with the works of the great Florentine artist, employed Michelangelo almost exclusively upon the façade and the sacristy of San Lorenzo. Michelangelo betook himself to the sculptures for the tomb during the short and stern pontificate of Adrian VI. ; but under Clement VII. was obliged to abandon them once more in order to carry out Leo's plans in Florence, which were adopted by the new Pope. About 1531 the Duke of Urbino at last obtained permission for Michelangelo to break off the works at San Lorenzo in order to finish the tomb which had been in hand so long ; it does not however appear that he was even then able to do much to it. At last, after the death of Clement he hoped to recover his liberty and to be able to fulfil his engagements after so much involuntary delay ; but Paul III. was hardly installed before he sent for him, received him with the utmost condescension, and begged him to devote his talents to his service. Michelangelo replied that it was impossible, that he was under a contract to complete the tomb of Julius II. Paul flew into a great rage and said, " This has been the wish of my heart for the last thirty years, and now that I am Pope it is not to be gratified. I will tear the contract in pieces, and I expect you to obey my orders." The Duke of Urbino complained and warmly upbraided Michelangelo with a breach of faith. The sculptor not knowing which to listen to, begged the Pope to let him finish the work which he had promised. He conceived the most pre-

posterous schemes for escaping from the friendly restraint of
Paul, among others to withdraw to Carrara, where he had
passed some quiet years in the midst of the marble mountains.   The Pontiff put an end to all discussions by issuing a
brief, dated September 18th, 1537, by which he declared
Michelangelo, his heirs and successors, freed from all obliga-
tions resulting from the different compacts respecting the
tomb.   This mode of settling matters could neither satisfy
the Duke of Urbino nor release Michelangelo. The discussion
was resumed and ended in an agreement that the tomb
should be finished as we now see it in the church of San
Pietro in Vincoli, and should be composed of the statue of
Moses, entirely finished by the hand of Michelangelo, of two
figures representing the one Active, the other Contemplative
Life, which were in an advanced condition and were to be
finished by Raffaello da Montelupo, of two other statues by
this master, of a Virgin after a drawing by Michelangelo, and
lastly of the recumbent figure of Julius, by Maso del Bosco.
Such is briefly the history of this monument, which was not
entirely completed till 1550, after having been a source of
actual torment to Buonarroti for half a century.

The Duke of Urbino was by no means satisfied, nor was
Michelangelo.   The figures originally intended to form part of
a colossal whole under the gigantic vault of St. Peter's appear
too large for their present position.   The prominence of the
statue of *Moses* perplexes the mind, and even creates the
idea that the monument is raised to the memory of the Hebrew
lawgiver rather than to that of the warrior-pontiff.   In fact,
the principal, if not the sole interest of the tomb, is centred
upon this statue.   It is this sublime work which remains
stamped upon the memory.   The *Moses* dwells amidst the
masterpieces of ancient and modern sculpture, an event with-

The Creation of Adam   [*Sistine Chapel*

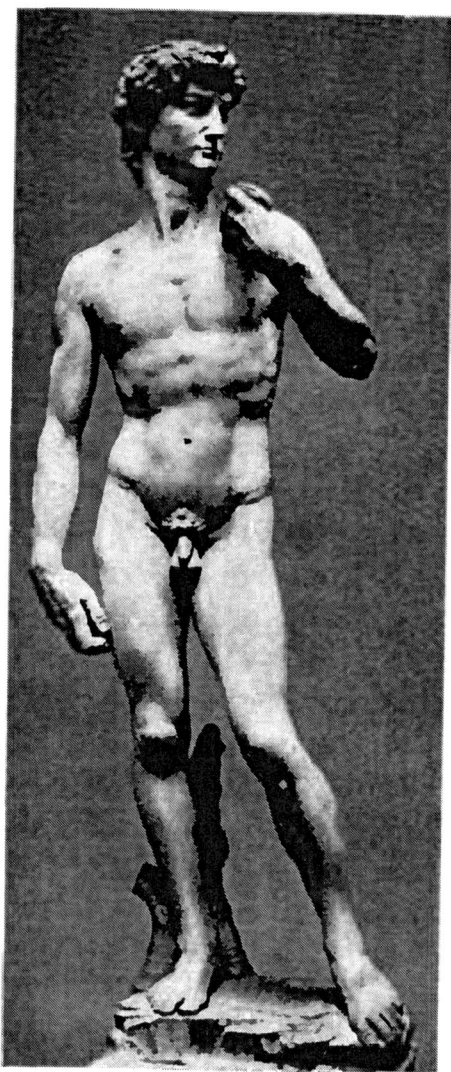

David   [*Florence*

out a parallel, the representative, if not wholly faultless, still
the most perfect, of an art unknown before. I will not speak
of the consummate technical knowledge which Michelangelo
reveals in the modelling of this statue; the Greeks had a
knowledge as well as he, but it was of another sort. Whence
comes it, however, that, despite some trifling imperfections,
which it were out of place either to defend or deny, and,
although this stern figure be far from attaining or pretending
to the serene and tranquil beauty which the ancients regarded
as the supreme limit of art,—whence comes it that even upon
a soul the most forewarned it produces an impression which
cannot be resisted? It is because it is more than human, and
it bears away the spirit into a world of thought and feelings,
which the ancients were less familiar with than ourselves.
Their voluptuous art, while raising the form of man to heaven,
kept down the soul upon the earth. The *Moses* of Michelangelo has seen God, has listened to His voice like thunder,
has preserved the terrible impression of that meeting upon
Sinai ; his unfathomable gaze is searching into the mysteries
which he sees in prophetic vision. Is it the Moses of the
Bible? I know not. Would Praxiteles and Phidias have
represented Lycurgus and Solon thus? We may boldly
answer, no. The lawgiver in their hands would have been
an embodiment of law ; they would have represented an abstract existence by a figure over whose harmonious beauty
no change could come. Moses is not only the lawgiver of a
people ; it is not thought alone which dwells beneath that
powerful brow ; he feels, he suffers, he lives in a moral world
to which Jehovah has admitted him, and although more than
human, he is still a man.

There only remain to be noticed three figures of importance
which were to have formed part of the tomb of Julius II.,

D

but which could not be displayed in the smaller monument in San Pietro in Vincoli.   Firstly, there is one of the statues of *Victory* nearly finished, which stands now in the council chamber of the Signory, then the two wonderful *Captives* which the Louvre is fortunate enough to possess.   These last are among the finest of Michelangelo's works, and there is, to my thinking, some evidence of their being those which were blocked out during his stay in Carrara, in the first outburst of his enthusiasm, long before the Monument had caused him so much anxiety and vexation.   One of these figures is by no means perfect, but the other has that delicate finish which he used to put to his early works.   For loftiness of style, boldness and grace of outline, suppleness and power of model, and for idealism of character, it will ever take its place among the most finished productions of the chisel.   These two works were first given by Michelangelo to Roberto Strozzi, who had received him in his house, and tended him in illness ; they were brought into France, and Francis I. made a present of them to Marshal Montmorency, who put them in his castle at Écouen.   They were conveyed afterwards to Poitou by Richelieu ; then they were taken to his house in the Faubourg du Roule, and put up for sale in 1793, and Lenoir purchased them for the Museum of French Monuments.   They are now in one of the rooms devoted to the sculptures of the Renaissance.

Now I must go back and take up the course of events at the point where I digressed, in order to dwell upon a work which, notwithstanding its importance, has occupied too large a place in the life of Michelangelo.   On his return from Bologna, at the beginning of 1508, he found Julius II. by no means cold in his feeling towards him, but preoccupied with new schemes.   He talked about his tomb no longer, but entirely about the rebuilding of St. Peter's, which he had put into Bramante's hands. Raphael was at this time beginning the frescoes in the Hall of the Signory, and the two biographers of Michelangelo, whose evidence upon this point must, it is true, be received with caution, agree in declaring that the architect of St. Peter's was jealous of the superiority of the Florentine sculptor. He was afraid that he would discover the mistakes which had been made in the new buildings and the malpractices of which he was not perhaps guiltless. In the hope, therefore, of compromising and ruining him by employing him on works to which he was not accustomed, he induced the Pope to entrust Michelangelo with the vault-paintings of the chapel which had been built under Sixtus IV. Julius caught at the idea. Buonarroti was summoned and ordered to begin at once. He had done no fresco work since the time of his apprenticeship with Ghirlandaio, and knew that it was not an easy thing to paint a vault. He excused himself, and proposed Raphael, saying that he was nothing but a sculptor and should fail in such a work. The Pope was inflexible, and on the 10th of May, 1508, Michelangelo began this vault, perhaps the most prodigious monument of human genius on record. Julius had ordered Bramante to construct the necessary scaffolding, but he set about it so clumsily that Michelangelo was obliged to dispense with his assistance and to do everything for himself. He summoned some of his old fellow-pupils from Florence, not, as Vasari, under the most strange misconception, asserts, because he knew nothing about the method of fresco-painting, which was familiar to all artists of that period, but because his fellow-workmen were more accustomed to it than himself, and he wanted assistance in so important a work. He was, however, so dissatisfied with their style, that he destroyed all they had done, and, if we may believe his biographer, shut himself up in the chapel without any assistant, grinding his own colours and preparing his own plaster. Thither he went at daybreak and never left till nightfall, sometimes even sleeping in his clothes upon the scaffolding, only allowing himself one light meal at the end of the day, and permitting no one a sight of what he was doing. Scarcely had he begun than unforeseen difficulties arose, which were on the point of making him give up the work entirely. The colours, even before they were dry, were covered with a mould, and he could not discover the cause. He went back to the Pope disheartened: " I warned your Holiness," he said, "that painting was not my art. All I have done is lost, and if you do not believe me, send some one to see it." Julius sent Giuliano da San Gallo, who saw that the misfortune was owing to the quality of the Roman lime, and that Michelangelo used his plaster too damp. Buonarroti resumed his work with the utmost eagerness, and in twenty months the first half was completed without another mishap.

The mystery in which Michelangelo shrouded himself had excited general curiosity. The objections of the painter had not prevented Julius from coming to see him several times, and, despite his great age, he had mounted right up to the platform by a bolt-ladder and with the help of Michelangelo's hand. He would wait no longer. He would have everybody share in his admiration without more delay. It was of no use for Michelangelo to object that the scaffolding would have to be rebuilt, and that he had not put the last touch to his work: the Pope would not hear a word, and the chapel was open to the public on All Saints' Day, November the 1st, 1509. " All Rome," says Vasari, "rushed to the Sixtine. Julius was there first, before the dust from the falling scaffolding was laid, and said mass in the chapel the same day."

The success was immense; Bramante, seeing that his vile plot, far from succeeding, had only increased the fame of Michelangelo, who had come forth in triumph from the snare which he had laid for him, begged the Pope to give Raphael the other half of the chapel to do. Julius, however, kept to his resolution, despite his desire to please the architect, and after a short interval Michelangelo resumed the painting of the vault; but rumours of these intrigues came to his ears; he went to the Pope with bitter complaints of Bramante's conduct towards him, and no doubt the coolness between him and Raphael dated from this time.

The second, and by far the most considerable part of the vault was not finished till 1512, and it is difficult to understand how Vasari could say that this enormous undertaking was finished in twenty months. He seems to have confused the dates, to have referred to the whole that which only applies to the first half. It is marvel enough that Michelangelo could finish so gigantic a work in four years; there is no need to excite still greater astonishment by trying to make out that it was completed in an utterly impossible space of time.

The impatience of Julius was so great that he almost fell out with Michelangelo a second time. The artist wanted to go to Florence on business, and went to ask for money. "When will you finish my chapel?" said the Pope. "As soon as I can," replied Michelangelo. "As soon as I can, as soon as I can—why, I'll pitch you off your scaffold," cried the irascible Pontiff, giving him a slight blow with his stick. Michelangelo went home, packed up his things, and was on

the point of starting off, when the Pope sent his favourite
Accursio to him with his apologies and 500 ducats.

Again Michelangelo could not finish his work as completely
as he wished. He wanted to touch it up when it was dry.
But when the scaffolding was once down, he contented himself
with leaving it as it was. He said that what was wanting
to the figures was immaterial. "You must put in a little
gilding," said the Pope. "My chapel will look poor."
"The people I have painted on it were poor," replied Michelangelo, and no alteration was made.

These paintings of the Sixtine vault are beyond description. How could one give any idea of those numberless and
sublime figures to those who have not quailed and trembled
in this temple of wonders? The unrivalled grandeur of
Michelangelo shines forth even in the chapel which contains
the pictures of Ghirlandaio, of Signorelli, which pale before
those of the Florentine, as the light of a lamp under that of
the sun. Raphael painted his wonderful *Sibyls* of the Pace
about the same time, and under the influence of what he had
seen in the Sixtine: compare them! He also, no doubt,
attained to the highest regions of art in some of his works,—
the *St. Paul* at Hampton Court,[1] the *Vision of Ezekiel*, the
Virgin of the Dresden Museum,—but what was the exception
with Sanzio was the rule with the great Buonarroti. Michelangelo had glimpses of a world which is not this. His daring
and unlooked-for flights of fancy are so far above and outside
the ordinary range of human thought, that they repel by
their very sublimity, and are far from captivating ordinary
minds like the marvellous and charming creations of the
painter of Urbino.

It is important however to combat the widespread opinion

---

[1] Now in the South Kensington Museum.

that Michelangelo comprehended only extravagant ideas,
and could only express them by exaggerated and contorted
movements. His figures possess the highest qualities of art,
originality, sublimity of style, breadth and skill in outline,
precision, and harmony of colour, and that character so striking in the Sixtine pictures, which precludes a thought of the
painter. That portentous sky seems as if it must have come
thus peopled with its giant forms, and it requires an effort
of thought to imagine a creator of so sublime a work. All
this is conceded, but he is refused the knowledge of grace, of
beauty in its youth and brightness, of form which expresses
tender and delicate feelings, such as the divine pencil of
Raphael has so wonderfully represented. I allow that Michelangelo took little pains to please, and that his stern genius
delighted only in the gravest thought; but I do not acknowledge that he was a stranger to grace and beauty, especially in
women. Not to mention the *Virgin* of the Academy in London,
or, in another style, the wonderful *Captive* of the Louvre;
without leaving the Sixtine, what more marvellous vision of
beauty could appear in dreams than that *Adam* opening his
eyes upon the light for the first time? What more chaste,
more graceful, more lovely than the youthful form of that *Eve*
bending towards her Creator and drawing from his half-open
lips the divine breath which gives her life? What is the
meaning of that work so full of terror? What is the meaning of that long unrolling of human destiny? Why did those
two beings whom we see beautiful and happy in the beginning people the earth with that passionate and restless race,
gigantic yet powerless? Ah! Greece would have made of
that vault an Olympus inhabited by forms happy and god-
like! Michelangelo has peopled it with beings grand and
unhappy, and this mournful poem of humanity is truer than

the marvellous fictions of ancient Poetry and Art. "Michelangelo," Condivi tells us, "was a special admirer of Dante. Moreover, he devoted himself diligently to reading the Holy Scriptures and the writings of Savonarola, for whom he always entertained great affection, retaining even the remembrance of his mighty voice." On the other hand, the native land of the great Florentine, the glorious Italy of the Renaissance, was on the eve of dissolution. Such studies, such memories, such mournful realities, may interpret the visions which passed through the mind of the great artist during the four years of almost complete solitude which he passed in the Sixtine. The precise meaning of his compositions will probably escape us, but so long as man exists, they will draw the spirit towards the dim world of fancy, and this is the end of art.

The year which followed the opening of the Sixtine, and which preceded the death of Julius, seems, like the two first of the Pontificate of Leo X., to have been among the happiest and calmest of Michelangelo's life. The old Pope loved him "with an anxiety and jealousy," says Condivi, "which he had for no one else about him." He honoured his integrity, and even that independence of character of which he had more than once had proof. Michelangelo, on his part, overlooked that rough treatment which was so promptly and perfectly atoned for. His sight, weakened by that four years' incessant work, compelled him to rest almost entirely. "The necessity," says Vasari, "for always looking upwards during the time of his work, had so weakened his sight, that for several months afterwards he could not see a drawing nor read a letter without holding it over his head." He enjoyed unrivalled fame in that period of semi-repose which succeeds a mighty effort. Probably all his thoughts at this time were centred upon his work for the tomb of his patron, which he had been compelled to abandon for a time; but Leo X. required him for something else. He was all-powerful in Florence, where, thanks to Julius and the league of Cambray, he had established his family in 1512, and he wanted to endow his country with monuments which should recall to the vanquished citizens of that glorious republic the magnificence of their former patrons, and thus make them forget the institutions which they had just lost a second time.

The church of San Lorenzo, which was built by Brunelleschi, and which was the burial-place of several members of the Pope's family, was unfinished; he resolved to complete the front. Several artists, among whom were San Gallo, the two Sansovinos, and Raphael, sent in plans for this important work; but Michelangelo's was successful, and he went to Carrara in 1515 to get the necessary marbles cut out.

Leo did not leave him there long at rest. Learning that there were marbles at Serravezza, in the highest part of the mountains of Pietra Santa, and on Florentine territory, which rivalled those from Carrara, he ordered Michelangelo to go and begin to work the quarries. The sculptor pointed out in vain the enormous expenditure which the opening of these quarries would involve: There were roads to carry right up the mountain, marshes to cross, and the marble was of an inferior quality. Leo would listen to nothing.

Michelangelo set out, opened the roads, got out the marble, and remained in this solitude from 1516 to 1521. The result of four years of the flower of his age and genius spent there was the transport of five columns, four of which remained on the sea-coast, and the fifth is at this day unused and lying among the rubbish in the Piazza di San Lorenzo.

Without wishing to deny all that the Arts owe to Leo X., his services must be accepted with some reserve. Accomplished, and of amiable manners, but crafty and blundering; always vacillating between France and the Emperor; ambitious above everything to find places for his family; and to counterbalance such faults, having neither the valour, nor the affection for Italy which Julius II. undeniably displayed, his political character can not, I think, be defended.

He had the merit of being the patron of Raphael, whose compliant and easy character pleased him, and who, thanks to his patronage, left the impress of a master-piece upon every moment of his short life. We must not forget that it was by heedless extravagance, and by a general traffic, that Leo encouraged the pleiad of artists which has cast such lustre upon his name. His obstinacy in employing Michelangelo despite his repugnance and entreaties, upon a work which his own versatility of character and the embarrassments of the Lombard war ought to have made him abandon, has doubtless robbed us of some wonderful works. Michelangelo might have finished the tomb of Julius, and we should now have a gigantic monument which would rival the greatest works of ancient sculpture.

Some expressions of Condivi show us into what a state of annoyance and discouragement Michelangelo was thrown by the instability of Leo, and the uselessness of such work. "On his return to Florence he found the ardour of Leo quite subsided; there he was for a long time filled with vexation, unable to do anything, having been hurried about from one scheme to another up to that time, to his intense disgust." It was, however, about this period, in 1520, that Leo ordered the tombs of his brother Giuliano and his nephew Lorenzo for the Sacristy of San Lorenzo, which he did not execute till ten years afterwards. He also ordered plans for the Laurentian Library, where the wonderful collection of manuscripts by Cosimo and Lorenzo the Magnificent, which had been dispersed during the troubles of 1494, were to be brought together. He was at Florence when the Academy of Santa Maria Nuova, of which he was an energetic member, resolved to bring the ashes of Dante from Ravenna to Bologna, and addressed that beautiful petition to the Pope, which Gori has preserved for us, bearing the signatures of the most celebrated men of the time, among others that of Michelangelo, with this memorial:—" I, Michelangelo, the sculptor, also supplicate your Holiness, and offer to execute a tomb worthy of the divine poet in a place of honour in the city." Leo did not entertain the idea favourably, and it was abandoned.

The Statue of *Christ on the Cross*, which had been ordered by Antonio Metelli, and which is in the Church of Santa Maria sopra Minerva, was probably executed during the rare sojourns which Michelangelo made in Rome during Leo's pontificate. So great had become his discouragement that he had it finished and set up by a Florentine sculptor named Federigo Frizzi, at the end of 1521. The statue of the *Christ*, one which bears marks of the highest finish and intelligence of all that came from the hands of Michelangelo, is in my opinion far from equalling other works of the great sculptor. It was, however, the rapidly-acquired celebrity of the work finished by Federigo Frizzi which decided Francis I. to send Primaticcio into Italy, under orders to copy for him the *Christ* of the Minerva, to order a statue from Michelangelo, and to put into his hands that flattering letter which is preserved in the precious collection at Lille.

Leo X. died on the 1st of December, 1521, a year after

Raphael. His successor, the humble and stern Adrian, knew nothing of painting except that of Van Eyck and Albrecht Dürer. His simple manners were in most striking contrast with the ostentatious habits of Leo. Under his pontificate all the great works were stopped in Rome and slackened in Florence. While Michelangelo was working quietly on the Laurentian Library, the grand age of Art was coming to an end. Raphael and Leonardo were dead, and their pupils were rapidly hurrying on a downward course. Character began to decline with talent, and Michelangelo, who had, so to speak, opened this great epoch, was destined to remain alone when all had gone, like those lofty peaks which are the first to receive the morning rays, and the last to lose the light, even when night is deepening and all about them is becoming dark.

CHAPTER IV.

ITALIAN AFFAIRS—DEFENCE OF FLORENCE—MICHELANGELO
AS AN ENGINEER—THE LEDA—SAN LORENZO—RETURN TO
ROME—THE LAST JUDGMENT—APPOINTED ARCHITECT OF
ST. PETER'S.

A.D. 1521 TO A.D. 1546.

JULIUS II. died without completely attaining his double
aim, the expulsion of foreigners from Italy and the
absorption of the different States of the Peninsula by
the Papal power. He increased his sway by diminishing the
power of Venice, but destroyed for ever one of the strongest
-bulwarks of Italian independence. The crafty policy of Leo
upheld the supremacy of the Church, but the indecision of
Clement VII. was not long in compromising the results
which had been obtained by the courage and skill of his two
illustrious predecessors.

Francis I. laid claim to Naples, the Emperor to Milan, and
Italy was once more a prey to all the devastating agents of
the most terrible of wars. The Constable of Bourbon did
not stop at Florence; it was the sack of Rome which the
Spanish and German hordes demanded, of Rome defenceless

and more brilliant than she had ever been. The republican party in Florence took advantage of the downfall and captivity of Clement VII. to drive out the Medici again. The name of Michelangelo is closely bound up with this supreme effort which his country made for the recovery of her independence, and to have been among her most useful and active defenders is not one of his least titles to renown.

When the events of 1527 occurred, Michelangelo had been in Florence for several years, employed on the works of San Lorenzo and the tomb of the Medici. He was then more than fifty years old. His character, which had always been impetuous, was not softened by age. Carrying his love of solitude almost to a mania, caring little for most of the men among whom he lived, as the sarcastic and offensive words which are attributed to him abundantly prove, he was never mixed up in party conflicts. There were reasons for his abstaining, apart from his character. His republican convictions made him detest the tyrannical and impotent rule of the later Medici; but his attachment to Lorenzo and the gentle remembrance which he had retained of him as a patron and friend made it difficult for him to enter the lists against his degenerate successors.

However, in the midst of his advancing career, and just as he had determined to devote himself more than ever to his art, events occurred which imperatively demanded a change in his resolves, and which gave a peculiar character to the second part of his life, by throwing him headlong into political struggles. The captivity of Clement VII. did not last long. Charles V. had just become reconciled to the Pope, and the re-establishment of the Medici was one of the principal stipulations of the Treaty of Barcelona. The

Florence government did not wait for the Pope to lay siege to the city before taking steps for its defence. The fortifications were inadequate and in a bad state. All eyes turned to Michelangelo. He was named Director and Commissioner-General of the Fortifications. His sympathy with the movement which gave liberty to Florence was perfect. Whatever his repugnance might be on personal grounds he did not think that genius absolved him from being an honest man, and he accepted.

The activity which he displayed on this occasion seems to have been prodigious. "He fortified the city at many points," says Vasari, "and surrounded San Miniato with stout bastions of chestnut and oak, not of the ordinary turf and brushwood. He even substituted bricks of animal hair and dung for the turf." In April and May he was at Leghorn, in June at Pisa, engaged in the citadel works and the Arno fortifications. The following month he was off to Ferrara, whither the Signory of Florence sent him to study the new style of fortification employed by Duke Alfonso. Again, in September, he was at Arezzo, directing the defences there.

The fortifications of Michelangelo, which Vauban studied and admired, still enclose the lovely church and the cypress trees of San Miniato ; they encircle the most charming of hills with a dark and sombre belt. I am not competent to judge of these ramparts as military works, but I have never seen them without thinking of the great man who constructed them, and who, when he might have been content with his reputation as an artist, determined to take part in his country's last struggle for liberty.

According to Vasari, Michelangelo remained almost continually in the fortress for the six months which preceded the siege, directing everything in person, and trusting in no one else. "When he did come down into the city it was to work *stealthily* on the San Lorenzo statues." This casual word of his biographer depicts the mental perplexities of Michelangelo better than the longest dissertation. He was compelled to fight against a Medici to satisfy his conscience and his judgment, and dared not allow the feelings to be seen which brought upon him an accusation of treason from an excited and suspicious people. So by a sort of compromise and to reassure his heart which protested against his actions, he only gave over the fight with Clement to push on the tombs of Lorenzo and Giuliano in secret.

Then sprung up disunion between the defenders of the city. The *condottiere*, Malatesta Baglioni, was appointed Commander-in-Chief. Rumours of treason were about among the soldiers. Some officers came to give Michelangelo warning. He went to the Signory, and laid bare the danger of the city ;—Malatesta was a traitor, there was still time to put everything right, but steps must be taken without delay. "Instead of thanks," says Condivi, " he only received insults from the Gonfaloniere Carduccio, who treated him like a man who was afraid and over-suspicious." He was disgusted at the injustice of Carduccio, and saw that the advice of the perfidious Malatesta was preferred to his own. Under such circumstances he could do nothing for the defence of the city. In the simple discharge of his duties he was exposing himself to the madness of the people, without advantage to any one. He left Florence with his pupil Mimi and his friend Ridolfo Corsini. He withdrew first to Ferrara and then to Venice, where he stayed for a short time.

The works for the defence of Florence had been carried on with so much skill and energy that the journey of Michel-

The Delphic Sibyl *Sistine Chapel*

[Face page 52

Lorenzo de Medici *Florence*

angelo was nothing but a series of ovations, which, do what he
would, he could not check. People saw in him not the artist
only but the defender of the independence of the Republic of
Florence. It was the manly character which he had displayed,
far more than his frescos and his statues, which won for him
that swift popularity and enthusiastic admiration which follow
upon public services. The Duke of Ferrara, who found him
out, despite all his pains to hide himself, carried him off almost
by main force to his palace, overwhelmed him with attentions
and with presents, showed him his pictures, and, among others,
his own portrait by Titian. "Immediately after his arrival,"
says Varchi, "Michelangelo withdrew quietly to Giudecca, to
escape from visits of ceremony which he detested, and to
enjoy his customary solitude." But the presence of such a
man in the city could not remain unknown. The Signory
sent two of their principal gentlemen to pay him a formal
visit, and to entreat his acceptance of everything which either
he or his friends might require. "This is a proof," says the
historian, " of Michelangelo's eminence, and of the admiration in which these illustrious men held such virtues."

His precipitate flight has been attributed to an excessive
and culpable prudence, without any consideration of his character and circumstances. This accusation will not bear
examination ; but, as it has been brought up again of late,
it must not be passed over in silence. There is no doubt
something unusual in this abrupt decision of Michelangelo ;
but he acted consistently with that character which is familiar
to us. Irritable, impetuous, quick in resolution, he took counsel
with no one but himself. His conduct in the midst of the
events which succeeded his departure and return, at a moment
of supreme peril, leaves no doubt as to the motives of his action.
The Signory had declared Buonarroti and his companions

E

traitors by a decree of September 30 ; but the people protested, and demanded that their Michelangelo should be given them. "The most earnest entreaties," Condivi says, "were addressed to him ; they begged him to consider his country's interests and not to give up the enterprise upon which he had embarked." Overcome by consideration for those who wrote to him, but mainly urged on by his love for his country, he asked for a safe conduct, and returned to Florence at the risk of his life.

The march of Clement across Tuscany was rapid. Perugia, Cortona, Arezzo opened their gates to him, and he arrived under the walls of Florence in the month of October. San Miniato commands the city, and the Pope's first object was to secure the position. Besides the bastions Michelangelo had mounted several pieces of cannon on the Campanile, which made great havoc among the besiegers. He conceived the idea of covering the bastions with mattresses and bales of wool. On his return he forthwith resumed his command, and conducted the defence for six months with the utmost energy. Unhappily there was dissension in the city. One part of the people, who had lost all virtues and taste for liberty under the enervating sway of the Medici, longed for them again. "Almost all the wealthy," wrote Busini to Varchi, "demanded their return, some out of ambition or folly, others out of servility." Francesco Ferrucci performed miracles at the head of a little army devoted to him. That bold and useful diversion, the heroic struggles of the people, whose incessant sorties left the besiegers no rest, were only able to break the fall of the last of the Italian republics which had kept the spirit and the letter of its institutions intact. Famine came to join the array of evils. At last Malatesta threw off the mask, opened the Roman gate, and brought the Imperialists into the city. It surrendered on the 12th of August, 1530. Although the terms of surrender had stipulated for a wide-extended amnesty, the most illustrious citizens of Florence were put to death, exiled, or robbed of their property. There was no doubt about Michelangelo's fate, had he been taken, for he was excluded from the amnesty along with certain of the defenders of the city. He hid himself, some say at a friend's, but more probably according to the family tradition, in the tower of S. Nicolas, beyond the Arno. There he remained for some time. The Pope's anger subsided. Clement wanted him to finish the San Lorenzo tombs, so he published an announcement that he would spare his life and forget the past.

During one of his visits to Ferrara, Michelangelo undertook to paint a picture for Duke Alfonso, in return for his hospitality, directly he got back to Florence; and during the siege he finished a *Leda*, which was destined for him. The duke was afraid that some harm might come to the picture during the troubles which followed the surrender of the city, and sent one of his suite to ask for it; but through the stupidity of the messenger, this painting found its way into France, instead of going to Ferrara. Vasari has preserved an account of the discussion which decided its fate, and which is another evidence at once of Michelangelo's irritability of temper and excellence of heart. "He received the gentleman graciously, and showed him a large painting, in which he had represented *Leda embracing Jupiter*, under the form of a swan. This noble personage said to him, "Oh, I don't think much of that!" "What style do you like, then?" said Michelangelo. "I am a merchant," replied the other," as if to let him see his contempt for Florentine industry. Michelangelo, thoroughly aware of this, replied

promptly, "Well, Mr. Merchant, you will make a bad bargain for your master to-day." He gave the magnificent
painting to his pupil, Antonio Mimi, who had been recom-
mended to him, and who had two marriageable sisters. Mimi
carried the work into France, along with some drawings, cartoons, and models which Michelangelo had given him. Most
of these treasures perished, like so many other beautiful
things which we have not been able to keep. The *Leda* was
bought by Francis I. and placed at Fontainbleau. It was
there up to the time of Louis XIV., when the prudish
Desnoyers had it defaced, and even gave orders to have it
burned. This order does not seem to have been executed,
for Mariette saw the picture reappear far on in the eighteenth
century, "but so damaged that only the canvas was left in
numberless places. The genius of a grand artist, however,
shows itself unmistakably, even through these disfigure-
ments. I have seen nothing of Michelangelo's so well
painted, according to my judgment. It seemed as if the
sight of Titian's works, which he had at Ferrara—the place
for which his own picture was destined—stimulated him to
adopt a better tone of colouring than that which was peculiar to him. However this may be, I saw this picture
restored by an ordinary artist, and it went into England,
where, no doubt, it had a great success.

This is another work of Michelangelo which seems to have
been irrecoverably lost. Waagen has found no trace in England of that ill-restored canvas of which Mariette speaks,
and which, according to Argenville and Piles, was actually
destroyed by fire. It is true that we are familiar with the
composition from the cartoon in the London Academy, which
has also been engraved. But the loss of that painting upon
canvas, according to the exact description of the precise

Mariette, and probably in oil, which would be a twofold exception to Michelangelo's ordinary work, is so much the more to be regretted, as the work was executed at the time when the Artist of the Sixtine was in the fulness both of his vigour and genius. The *Leda* of the London cartoon recalls the *Night* of the San Lorenzo Tomb. There is an atmosphere of rude and forbidding voluptuousness, but nothing in common with the obscene figures which the decline of ancient art has bequeathed to us. Under the sway of Neo-platonic sentiments the painters of the Renaissance interpreted the story of *Leda* as the union of Man with Nature—the seduction of the intellectual being by the sensual. So Leonardo da Vinci and Correggio treated the subject; and it would have been highly interesting to be able to compare their works with that of their omnipotent rival.

Clement VII. pardoned Michelangelo his share in the defence of Florence only upon condition that he would finish the San Lorenzo tombs. It required all the firm friendship of the Pope to defend the sculptor against the hatred of Alexander de' Medici. Deceived in his most cherished hopes, compelled to be a passive and helpless spectator of the triumph of a cause which he detested, irritated at the dissensions of his party, which had brought about a defeat which his efforts could only delay, Michelangelo seems at this time to have become the melancholy victim of a disordered mind. His health was so seriously affected that the Pope issued a brief forbidding him, under pain of excommunication, all work in painting or sculpture, except that which related to the sacristy of San Lorenzo. Some months before his pupil, Antonio Mimi, wrote, " Michelangelo seems to me fagged and falling away. We don't think he can live

long, if he doesn't take care of himself; it's all through hard
work, scanty and bad food, and want of sleep. For the
last month he has been subject to headache and giddiness.
He oughtn't to be allowed to work in the Sacristy all the
winter, and he might finish the Virgin in the little room at
the side." Alexander asked him to make plans for the construction of a citadel, but he refused flatly to work for him.
This prince was a mulatto bastard of Clement VII., or,
according to others, of Lorenzo II. It is said that the irritated artist uttered those cutting words—which apply to
many other members of that degenerate race, as well as to
this monster—that "the Palace of the Medici ought to be
pulled down, and a piazza built upon the site, to be called
the Mules' piazza."

Michelangelo had not, so to speak, touched his chisel for
the last fifteen years. He set to work on the Tombs of San
Lorenzo with a sort of fury so great that by the end of 1531
the two female figures were finished, and the others far
advanced. There was an idea of placing four tombs in the
chapel, and it is probable that the one for Lorenzo the
Magnificent was included in this first scheme, which Clement VII. rejected, and confined himself to those of Giuliano,
Duke of Nemours, brother of Leo X.; and of Lorenzo, Duke
of Urbino, son of Peter, and father of Catharine de' Medici.
The chapel which contains these monuments is in the form
of a square, surmounted by a cupola. Michelangelo has
given many specimens of this severe and cold style in other
parts of San Lorenzo, in the numerous palaces which he
built, and, the most perfect, in St. Peter's at Rome. At the
head of the chapel is the altar; opposite to it a *Virgin and
Child*, one of his finest works, and two figures, which are
probably to a great extent by the hands of his pupils, Rafaello

da Montelupo and Fra Giovan Agnolo, who helped him in this great work; on either side, the full height of the wall, the two statues of Giuliano and Lorenzo.

There is nothing in this purely white and cold chapel to favour emotion; yet, who could look upon the statues of Giuliano or Lorenzo, the four allegorical figures which, two by two, adorn the sarcophagi, without being strongly and deeply moved? Michelangelo did not dwell upon the likenesses of his originals. In the tomb of Julius II., Rachel and Leah represent the active and contemplative life: in that of the Medici, the figures of Giuliano and Lorenzo personify thought and action. The four allegorical figures, *Dawn* and *Twilight*, *Day* and *Night*, recall the principal phases and the rapid course of man's destiny. The two figures of Giuliano and Lorenzo are sitting. Giuliano is young, dignified, and bold: he is in armour, and is resting his commander's bâton on his knee. Lorenzo is plunged in gloomy meditation; his head, full of thought, is supported by his hand; the finger upon the lips seems as if it would stop even the murmur of the breathing. Is it upon the ruins of Florence that he is fixing his eyes in that absorbed and fathomless gaze? What words can utter the majesty and power of that statue of Day—the Titanic beauty of that of Night—the pensive grace of the Dawn, opening her eyes in sadness upon a world of suffering? The tongue is powerless to utter the thoughts which the art portrays; but the world did not hesitate for a moment about the meaning of those figures; it gave the name of *Il Pensieroso*, the *Thoughtful*, to the statue of Lorenzo. The figure of *Night* made so powerful and universal an impression that a crowd of poets hastened to celebrate it. The stanza attributed to Strozzi is well known:

> [1] La *Notte*, che tu vedi in sì dolci atti
> Dormire, fù da un *Angelo* scolpita
> In questo sasso; e, perchè dorme, ha vita:
> Destala, se no 'l credi, e parleratti.

Michelangelo replied in the following verses, perhaps the most beautiful he ever wrote, which bear witness to the trouble of heart and mind in which he conceived and finished this most perfect piece of sculpture:

> [2] Grato mi è il sonno, e più l' esser di sasso:
> Mentre che il danno e la vergogna dura,
> Non veder, non sentir m' è gran ventura;
> Però non mi destar; deh parla basso!

The six statues which compose these two monuments—the admirable *Madonna*, which, with the two figures executed by his pupils, complete the ornaments of the Sacristy of San Lorenzo—are the consummation of the sculptor's skill in Michelangelo. All his knowledge, all the magnificence of his style, the exuberance of his imagination, the patience, the reasoning power which he brought to the execution of his boldest and most unlooked-for inventions, the new character, true and yet superhuman, which he put into his figures, that remarkable combination of qualities which made of the Florentine the giant of modern art,—all these appear perfected in this monument. The figures of San Lorenzo are not completely finished, as is the case in all the statues which he executed during the second part of his life. As

---

[1] This *Night*, whom thou seest slumbering in such a sweet abandon, was sculptured by an *Angel* in this marble; she is alive, although asleep: if thou wilt not believe it, wake her, she will speak.

[2] Sweet to me is slumber, and still sweeter to be in marble. Not to see, not to feel, is happiness in these days of baseness and dishonour. Wake me not then, I pray thee, but speak low.

he advanced in years his disposition to be impatient, at least
as far as works of art are concerned, became more marked.
Exulting in the beauty of form, jealous sometimes of its most
minute details, as may be seen in the torso and marvellous legs
of the *Night*, and in the whole figure of the *Dawn*, he
has only blocked-out some of his most beautiful works; and
in those he most nearly completed, he often left unfinished
some secondary parts, the completion of which would have
added little to the expression of his thought. His aim was
to speak, to strike, to convince. No man took less pains
to please in little ways, or cared less to shut the mouths of
fools. When he had said enough he was silent; and so he
subdues rather than fascinates. With his all-powerful hand
he drags the spirit into the lofty region where he dwells; but
it does not follow him without reluctance and a thrill of
terror. The sentiments which he evokes are not due solely
to that which is strange and unfamiliar in his works; but to
their intrinsic character, to the thought which directs them,
and to that special inspiration which, no doubt, Orcagna,
Masaccio, Ghiberti, Donatello, at first received, but which
finds its most perfect organ in the originator of the Medici
Chapel. It has been asked why Michelangelo, knowing as
he did know so much of ancient art, departed so far from it.
From the time of his early studies in the gardens of San
Marco to his extreme old age he never failed in his devotion
to it. His admiration for the torso of the Belvedere is well
known,—so great was it as to give rise to a story of his later
days, that he became blind, and used to be led close to this
famous marble that he might pass his feeble hands over its
form. For my part, I ask myself how he could have ex-
pressed his thoughts if he had followed too closely the traditions of ancient art. His manner of representing the

human form, so different, no doubt, from Greek conception, was not due solely to that natural impetuosity which carried him wildly away over the smooth and rhythmical lines of an art which had become sacred. Ghiberti and Donatello, despite all the elegance and delicacy of their chisel, are no nearer to those lines than he. But new thoughts required a new language for their utterance. It is something more which Michelangelo gives to his figures than that abstract spirit of the ancients, that vague glimmer which draws the soul on to a sense of actual perfection by hovering softly about perfect shapes. It is a new soul, an individual soul of later birth—passionate, suffering—which stirs those marble forms; unfettered, full of life and action, athirst for the infinite; she thinks, she joys, she suffers, and, although confined to narrow limits, she finds means to give utterance to her feelings and emotions.

Michelangelo returned to Rome in 1532. The Pope commissioned him to finish the paintings of the Sixtine, by executing two vast frescoes for the ends of the chapel, the *Last Judgment*, and the *Fall of the Rebel Angels*. On the death of Clement VII., in 1534, two years after, as the paintings were not begun, and as Michelangelo was very busy with the mausoleum of Julius II., whose "ashes," he said, "had been waiting too long," he tried to get released from his engagement. However, Paul III. loaded him with civilities, arranged "the tragedy of the tomb"—to use Condivi's words—with the Duke d'Urbino, and won over Michelangelo to finish Clement's plan at his expense. The artist and the Pope, however, very nearly fell out at the beginning. Paul wanted to remove the arms of Julius II., which were in the chapel, and to put up his own instead. Michelangelo objected, saying "That it was not right; that this honour was due to Julius and Clement." "Paul III.," adds Vasari, "far from being annoyed by this liberty, was full of respect for a man who had the courage to oppose him."

Clement's idea was that the *Fall of the Rebel Angels* ought to commence the vast cycle of the Sixtine compositions, and with the *Last Judgment* to form the celestial prologue and epilogue to the drama of humanity which was represented upon the chapel-vault. But the idea was not entirely carried out. Michelangelo had, indeed, already made several studies for the *Fall of the Angels,* and even a sketch, which the assistant who ground his colours copied in the Church of the Trinita de' Monti. He confined himself however to the *Last Judgment,* and the artist almost immediately undertook the painting of that immense composition, which was to cost him eight years of incessant toil. The *Last Judgment* was begun, at least as far as regards the cartoons, in 1533, but was not finished till 1541. The public was able to gaze on this grand fresco on Christmas Day of this year. It has been said that this was more the work of a sculptor than of a painter. It has been observed too, that the composition is divided into three distinct zones, without regard to unity; that the groups too, are not well connected with each other, and do not move in proper perspective; that Michelangelo, notwithstanding his grand qualities as a painter, his knowledge of form, model, and foreshortening, his broad, bold, and deep colouring, nevertheless excels in compositions where the number of persons represented is small, or in isolated figures; and lastly, that in many respects the *Last Judgment* is inferior to the paintings on the Sixtine vault. All this is true. But it is also true that this work is unique; that it is not to be judged by any comparison, but as one of those unheard-of efforts of the human mind which terrify and subdue, in defiance of all criticism. Nowhere else has Michelangelo fallen so decidedly towards that side to which he always inclined; nowhere has he shown less care to please and captivate; nowhere has he brought together a greater mass of difficulties, of forced positions, and exaggerated movements, or taken such liberties with form, motion, and posture—a sort of rhetoric of his art which was destined to plunge his followers into such monstrous excesses. Never did he soar to such heights as in this fresco, and especially in the paintings of the vault; and one may well believe that the Sixtine will remain the most wonderful monument of modern art.

There are hardly any details of the eight years which Michelangelo spent in the completion of his work. More alone, more gloomy than ever, always in face of those terrible creations of his mind, intoxicated with the strong overflowing of his thought,—what dreams, what chimeras, what terrors must have crowded upon his imagination! At times he was the victim of despair. One day he was injured by a fall from a scaffold; he went back and shut himself up—he longed for death. His doctor, Baccio, anxious at not seeing him, had the greatest difficulty to get at him; he insisted on nursing him, and brought him round. Strange and painful problem, this man! Stern, reserved, yet good and sensitive, he seems in this work to have forgotten his heart! His bold fancy, ever insatiable, ever in full flight, penetrated the realms of unfathomable mystery till dizzy with its very soaring, and saw nothing but horrors there! The Christ of the *Last Judgment* is neither the Christ of the Gospel nor of Michelangelo; it is nothing but an avenging and terrible God. I see, indeed, the angels, the saints, the elect; but their songs are drowned by shrieks of despair, and by the wailings of the damned. There is no day of pardon—no, not of justice there; it is the day of vengeance and of wrath,—*Dies iræ, dies illa!*

The *Last Judgment* produced a marvellous effect, and, as might be expected, also gave rise to a host of adverse criticisms. That final catastrophe of the world, with its nude figures and forced positions, its developments of muscle and form, its giant shapes, its forgetfulness of Christian sentiment, seems to have been severely blamed by several contemporaries, and even friends, of Michelangelo, among others by Aretino, who wrote to Ænea Vico that "this painting might give the artist a place among the Lutherans." As to the Pope, he was not offended, and took a more lively view of things. One day, as he was going to visit the works in the Sixtine, acccompanied by his Master of the Ceremonies, Biagio da Cesena, he asked him what he thought of this painting. Biagio replied that he thought it was a deplorable thing to put so many figures which made a shameless exhibition of their nakedness, in so sacred a place; the proper place for them was a bathing-house or a beer-shop, not the Pope's chapel. Michelangelo heard of it, and when he was alone he put in a likeness of the unfortunate master of the ceremonies among the damned, under a representation of Minos. The resemblance was so striking that the story soon got all over the city. Biagio went to the Pope with his grievances, who asked him where Michelangelo had put him. "In hell," he replied. "Alas!" rejoined Paul, laughing; "if he had only put you in purgatory, I could have got you out; but as you are in hell I can do nothing for you. My power doesn't reach so far. *Nulla est redemptio!*"

Julius III. and Marcellus II. respected the work of the great artist, but Paul IV. wanted to efface the *Last Judgment* as soon as he became Pontiff. It was only with great difficulty that he was induced to revoke the order which he had actually given. "Tell the Pope," replied Michelangelo to some one who was speaking of the Pontiff's dissatisfaction, "not to trouble himself with such a cause of distress, but to do something towards reforming mankind, a much easier thing than correcting pictures." Paul confined himself to commissioning Daniele da Volterra to *dress* the figures which injured his scruples, as he had already dressed Raphael's Isaiah. The painter executed his task to the satisfaction of the Pontiff, and got the surname of *braghettone—(breeches-maker,)* for his pains.

Gregory XIII., no less scrupulous than Paul IV., conceived the idea of substituting a composition of Lorenzo Sabbatini for the grand work of Michelangelo ; and later on the fanatical Clement XIII. made Stefano Pozzi finish the work which Daniele da Volterra began.

This fresco was not destined to be the last of Michelangelo's paintings. Paul III. had built the chapel which still bears his name in the interior of the Vatican. He commissioned Michelangelo to paint two pictures in it— the *Crucifixion of St. Peter* and the *Conversion of St. Paul.*

These frescoes were not finished till much later, probably in 1549, that is to say, a short time before the death of Paul, and when Michelangelo was 75 years old. This work had tried him greatly. "Painting, and especially fresco," says Vasari, "is not fit for old men." Although these two works are now in bad condition, the Sixtine painter is to be recognized in them, but rather by his faults than his excellences:

the inspiration is not sustained; the drawing, bold and clever as always, is unnecessarily constrained; and, as it is useless to conceal the fact, they bear marks of that feebleness of age which Michelangelo was free from more than any other man, but which no one entirely escapes.

The activity of Michelangelo did not however slacken, but was employed upon objects more suited to his age. Paul III., who was busy about the fortifications of the Borgo, required his advice. Michelangelo gave an opinion entirely opposed to that of San Gallo, who flew into a rage, and finished by telling him that he might be able to meddle with sculpture and painting, but understood nothing about fortifications. Michelangelo replied that he did not lay great store by his painting, but had not been very unsuccessful in the Florence defences. He reproached his opponent sharply for the blunders which he had made; and defended his own scheme so triumphantly, that the Pope abandoned San Gallo's to adopt it. Finally, at the death of San Gallo, in 1546, Michelangelo was appointed architect of St. Peter's. About this time it was that he received a commission to construct the buildings of the Capitol, and the admirable entablature of the Farnese Palace, the most inspired of his architectural works. Not being able to paint any longer, he commenced the *Descent from the Cross* as a recreation, and " because mallet work was necessary for his health." The work is to be seen in an unfinished state behind the high altar in Florence Cathedral.

Notwithstanding his advanced age, he was still so vigorous that Blaise de Vigenère, who saw him at work somewhere about this time, speaks of him thus: " I saw him when he was past sixty, and moreover not one of the strongest of men, strike off more scales of marble in one quarter of an hour than

three young marble cutters would have done in three or four—
a thing almost incredible to anyone who did not see it ; and he
set to with such force and fury that I thought the whole work
must go to pieces. He brought to the ground big pieces
three or four fingers thick with a single blow, so precisely
on his mark that if he had struck ever so little wide of
it he would have been in danger of ruining the whole,
because marble cannot be repaired afterwards like clay or
stucco."

CHAPTER V.

A.D. 1521 TO A.D. 1547.

MICHELANGELO worked up to his latest days on the *Descent from the Cross*, and on a *Pietà*, of which Vasari speaks, but of which nothing is known. He did not, however, undertake any other work in painting or sculpture. He was growing old. The time of great creations was gone. He was destined to consecrate his prodigious activity henceforth to the immense labour of managing the building of St. Peter's, and to other architectural works. I did not wish to interrupt the account of the longest part of his life, of which his works of art are the characteristic and principal events, to study closely the feelings which he has unfolded, with too sparing a hand, in his verses and letters which have been preserved, and upon which his ardent and pure attachment for the Marchioness of Pescara sheds an unlooked-for light. The half-concealed form of this noble lady completes that of the great Florentine, and it is not without pleasure that we find his heart, which seemed to have slumbered for more than sixty years, animated with a life no less powerful than his genius.

The poetic talent of Michelangelo is genuine, but has been too highly rated. Pindemonte calls the artist of the Sixtine "the man of four souls." To be wholly just we must acknowledge, as M. Vitet has done in a very judicious notice, that one of these souls of the great sculptor was "less richly endowed than its sisters." Graceful imagery, but more especially vigorous and nervous thought, abound in his verses. . . . He has put his mark on everything that he has touched; yet it is more as a comment upon his life and a revelation of his thoughts and innermost feelings, than for their literary and poetic merit, that they seem to me to deserve attention. The verses of Michelangelo belong to every period of his long career. From his first stay in Florence after his return from Rome he wrote them. Those on the back of his first sketch of the *David* in the Louvre are a proof of this; and we know from Condivi, that after finishing the statue of the Piazza of the Signory he remained for some time without doing any sculpture work, and was wholly devoted to the study of the Italian poets and orators, and to writing sonnets for his own amusement. Condivi assures us that Michelangelo "loved not only human beauty, but every beautiful thing—a beautiful horse, a dog, or landscape, forests and mountains." . . . I will not linger upon his love verses; I do not believe in them. If Michelangelo had loved, there would remain other proofs of that love than feeble imitations of Petrarch. . . . Pure in character from his youth, Michelangelo was devoted to his art. . . . "I have often," says Condivi, "heard him discuss the subject of love, and have learned from men who were present that he never spoke of it in other language than we find in Plato. I do not know what Plato says, but I do know very well that I was on most intimate terms with Michelangelo, and never heard from his lips any words but such as were becoming, and likely to check the ill-regulated desires which spring up in the bosoms of the young." . . . It is only in those of his poems which relate directly to his art that we discover the powerful and lofty thought of Michelangelo. I should like to quote as an example only one of his effusions, which seems to me one of his most ample and best inspirations: " There was given me at my birth, as an assurance of my vocation, that sense of the beautiful, my guide and my light in two arts ; but, believe me, it is this alone which raises my eyes to that height which I strive so eagerly to reach in painting or in sculpture. Leave more rash and grosser spirits to search only in the material for a beauty which raises and transports loftier souls even unto heaven. Eyes so weak cannot be lifted from mortal forms upwards towards God, or reach that point to which Divine favour alone can direct them."

In his way, however, Michelangelo was destined to love. It is his love for a woman, and the passionate remembrance of her which he retained to extreme old age, which fills up and brightens the closing period of his life. . . . The gentle yet stately form of the Marchioness of Pescara remains shrouded in a sort of mystery. Researches, and recently discovered documents, however, throw some light upon this noble lady and her relations to Michelangelo. Vittoria Colonna, Marchioness of Pescara, was born at Marino, an ancient fief of her family, in 1490. Her father, Fabrizio Colonna, had embraced the cause of the House of Aragon, and it was through the instrumentality of the young king Ferdinand that Vittoria was betrothed at four years of age to Ferdinand d'Avalos, Marquis of Pescara, whose family, of Castilian origin, had settled in the kingdom of Naples. She received that severe and romantic education which gives so special a character to the women of the sixteenth century. A touch of pedantry in them did not exclude either grace or tenderness, and we may pardon their Latin for the sake of the vigour and loftiness of their sentiments.

Vittoria was sought in marriage by the greatest personages of the time, among others by the Dukes of Savoy and Braganza; but she had grown up with the young Ferdinand. His taste had confirmed the choice of his family, and, as she herself says in one of her sonnets, immediately she knew him " her heart proscribed all other feeling." She married the Marquis of Pescara in 1507. Neither of them was more than seventeen years old. The marriage of these young people was celebrated with great pomp. They passed several years of even and perfect happiness in a villa which belonged to them upon the island of Ischia. However, they had no children, and inaction was irksome to the young marquis. Julius II. had just drawn Francis of Aragon into his league against France. Pescara offered his services, which were accepted. He was appointed a cavalry general directly he joined the army. He took part in the battle of Ravenna, and performed prodigies of valour against Gaston de Foix. Wounded and a prisoner, he was taken to Milan, as well as the Cardinal de' Medici, afterwards Pope Leo X. . . . During his captivity he composed his dialogues upon Love, which he dedicated to his wife as a proof of the faithfulness of his feeling.

For twelve successive years husband and wife saw each other only at rare intervals, and almost by stealth. Pescara held most important commands in the armies of Charles V.; as his reputation increased, his military duties became more urgent and absorbing. Vittoria, on her part, passed these long years of premature widowhood partly at Ischia, partly at Naples, engrossed in her love, and seeking no distraction save study and the hardest reading. . . . At the battle of Pavia, Pescara directed those famous charges which drove back the French cavalry and decided the victory. He was severely wounded, and after lingering for some time died in 1525. Vittoria set out for Milan, as soon as she heard of the danger, but the fatal news reached her at Viterbo. She returned to Naples, where she remained for seven years, plunged in the gloom of despondency. . . .

At the death of the Marquis of Pescara Vittoria was only thirty-five years old. She was in all the bloom of a beauty, which has been celebrated by her contemporaries. Several princes and illustrious personages sought her hand. She entrenched herself in the invariable reply, "that if the choice had been given her she would have died with her husband; that he lived, and would ever live, in her remembrance." It was in the midst of her despair that her religious convictions, the source of the inspiration of her *Rime Spirituale*, were born, and under circumstances which deserve narration.

For several years the ideas of the Reformation had been making great progress in Italy. . . . The Spaniard Valdez, whom Charles V. had ennobled for his military services, and whom he had employed on several diplomatic missions to Germany, had brought back thence to Naples the doctrines of Luther. He was well informed, of engaging conversational power, and soon became the centre of an association composed of a small number of persons belonging to the higher classes. Among these were several ladies, and, according to the historian Giannone, Vittoria Colonna herself. . . .

I do not, however, think that there is reason to conclude that Vittoria—and consequently Michelangelo—did, more or less secretly, abandon the Church and embrace the Reformed religion. Their religious poems, it is true, preserve no trace of Catholic legend. Christianity is there in all its simplicity, carried back to fundamental and primitive dogma. The ideas of the inability of man to do right, of justification by faith, of Christ as a Mediator—upon which the Reformers particularly insist—are to be met with in every line. But these ideas belong to St. Augustine, as well as to Luther and Calvin. . . .

Vittoria came to Rome in 1538. It is supposed that her earliest relations with Michelangelo date from this time, and that it was in the first outburst of grateful affection that he wrote to her,—

"I am going in search of truth with uncertain step. My heart, floating unceasingly between vice and virtue, suffers and finds itself failing, like a weary traveller wandering on in the dark.

"Ah! do thou become my counsellor. Thy advice shall be sacred. Clear away my doubts. Teach me in my wavering how my unenlightened soul may resist the tyranny of passion unto the end. Do thou thyself, who hast directed my steps towards heaven by ways of pleasantness, prescribe a course for me."

This first stay of Vittoria at Rome was not of long duration. More and more weary of the world, she retired to the Convent of St. Catherine, at Viterbo, where she found her learned and pious friend, Cardinal Pole. She divided her time between this retreat and Rome, where she settled permanently during the last years of her life. She had founded a retreat there for poor young girls, and devoted the time which was left from useful works to study and to Michelangelo. . . .

Master Francesco d'Ollanda, the architect and illuminator, had been sent into Italy by the Portuguese Government to study art. He wrote the account of his journey; this account contains some passages relating to Michelangelo and Vittoria, too characteristic not to be quoted verbatim :—

"Among the number of days that I passed thus in this capital (Rome)," says Master Francesco, "there was one, it was a Sunday, when I went to see, as was my wont, Messer Lactantius Toloméo, who had become friendly with Michelangelo. . . . They told me at his house that he had left word for me that he would be at Monte Cavallo, in the Church of San Silvestro, with Madam the Marchioness Pescara, to hear a reading from the Epistles of St. Paul; away I went then to Monte Cavallo. . . . She made me sit down, and when the reading was over she turned to me and said, 'One ought to be able to make presents to those who can be grateful, and so much the more as after I have given I shall have as great a share as Francesco d'Ollanda after he has received. Here, So-and-so! go to Michelangelo's, and tell him that Messer Lactantius and I are in this chapel, which is nice and fresh, and that the church is closed and pleasant. Ask him if he will be good enough to come and lose a part of the day with us, that we may have the benefit of gaining it with him; but don't tell him that Francesco d'Ollanda, the Spaniard, is here.' After some moments of silence we heard a knock at the door. . . . It was he. The marchioness rose to receive him, and remained standing for some time, until she placed him between herself and Messer

Lactantius. I sat a little apart. She spoke of one thing and another with much intelligence and grace, without ever touching upon the subject of painting, so as to make sure of the great painter. . . . At last she said, 'It's a well-known fact that a man will always be utterly beaten if he tries to attack Michelangelo on his own ground. . . . As for you (she said to him), I do not think you less praiseworthy for the way in which you can isolate yourself, and avoid our trivial talk, and to refuse to paint for every prince who asks you.'

" 'Madam,' says Michelangelo, 'perhaps you give me more than my deserts. . . . I can assure your Excellency that even his Holiness annoys me sometimes, by asking me why I do not show myself more often. Then I say to his Holiness that I prefer working for him after my own fashion than spending a whole day in his presence, as some others do.'

" 'Happy Michelangelo!' I exclaimed, on hearing this. 'Only Popes, of all princes, could pardon such an offence.'

" 'It is just such offences,' said he, 'that kings ought to overlook.' Then he added, 'I can tell you that the work I am responsible for gives me so much liberty that sometimes it happens while I am talking with the Pope, that without thinking I put on my old hat, and talk freely to his Holiness. However, he doesn't kill me for it.' . . .

" But Vittoria wants to accomplish her end, and make Michelangelo talk about painting. 'Should I ask Michelangelo,' she said to Lactantius, ' to relieve my doubts about painting, I hope he won't box my ears, as he usually does, to prove that great men are reasonable and not eccentric.'

" 'If your Excellency,' replied Michelangelo, 'will ask of

me anything that is worth offering to her, she shall be obeyed.

"The Marchioness continued, smiling, 'I want very much to know what you think of Flemish painting, for it seems to me more devout than the Italian.'

"'Flemish painting, madam,' said Michelangeolo, 'will generally please any devout person more than that of Italy. The latter will never bring a tear to the eye, while the Flemish will make many a one flow ; and this result is due not to the force or merit of the painting, but simply to the sensibility of the devout. Flemish painting will always seem beautiful to women, especially to the very old or very young, also to monks and nuns, and some noble spirits which are deaf to true harmony . . . It is only to works which are executed in Italy that the name of true painting can be given, and that is why good painting is called Italian. Good painting is in itself noble and religious. Nothing elevates a good man's spirit, and carries it farther on towards devotion, than the difficulty of reaching that state of perfection nearest to God which unites us to Him. Now good painting is an imitation of His perfection, the shading of His pencil, a music in fine, a melody ; and it is only a refined intellect which can appreciate the difficulty of this. That is why good painting is so rare, and why so few men can get near to or produce it . . . It is a fact that if Albrecht Dürer, a man of fine and delicate touch, or Francesco d'Ollanda, wanted to deceive me, and were to try and counterfeit or imitate a work so as to make it appear from Italy—well ! he might produce a good, indifferent, or bad work, but I give you my word that I should very soon tell that it was not painted in Italy or by an Italian.'"

Michelangelo was not long to enjoy the society of his noble

friend. Vittoria fell ill at the beginning of 1547. She was taken to the house of a relative, Giulia Colonna. Her condition rapidly became alarming, and she succumbed at the end of February of the same year. Michelangelo was present at her death. "He was mad with grief," says Condivi. " When she was dead he imprinted a kiss upon her hand, and bitterly regretted afterwards that he had not ventured to leave the like token of his love upon her brow."

CHAPTER VI.

ST. PETER'S AND THE SAN GALLISTS—DEATH OF URBINO—URGED
TO RETURN TO FLORENCE, BUT REMAINS AT ROME TO DIE—
FUNERAL—SKETCH OF HIS CHARACTER, MODE OF LIFE, AND
PERSONAL APPEARANCE—HIS PLACE IN HISTORY.

A.D. 1547 TO 1563.

MICHELANGELO survived Vittoria sixteen years.
Although he was employed successively by Popes
Julius III., Paul IV., and Pius IV. on the works of the Villa
Giulia, on the fortifications, and several of the gates of Rome,
on the construction of bridges, churches, and monuments, yet
he devoted himself almost entirely to St. Peter's, which he
was anxious to complete before his death. Old age laid its
hand upon him without breaking him down, and he remained
active and upright to the extreme limits of the age of
man. Years did not tell upon his mind more than upon his
body. He was upwards of four score years old when he
made most of the calculations for the dome of St. Peter's,
and the beautiful model which is preserved in the chamber
of San Gregorio, above the Clementine chapel. His opinions
do not seem to have been any longer contradictory. After

having obstinately refused the friendly and flattering attentions which Duke Cosmo lavished upon him, he seems, it is true, at the close of his life to have pardoned him for being the ruler of his country ; but although several times he seriously entertained the idea of returning to die in Florence, he always excused himself with the duke, on the score sometimes of his great age, sometimes of his works ; and we may well believe that the sore feelings of the battered old republican confirmed him in his determination not to leave Rome.

The increasing decline of art, and the first excesses of his disciples, did not unsettle his ideas. We know with what admiration and with what severity he spoke of Titian, after he had been with Vasari to see him at the Belvedere.

During those long years of decline, which saw the springs of life decreasing day by day, and his enthusiasm—that heaven-sent frenzy which makes everything easy to youth—flickering and going out, he preserved a settled silence upon his innermost feelings. He gave no sign of what he was suffering in a solitude peopled but just now with the phantom forms of his own genius ; and though still filled with an ardent and sacred love, became yet more desolate and gloomy than ever by the death of Vittoria. He spoke of himself with haughty pride : " For myself, in all my sufferings I have at least this satisfaction, that no one can read in my face the story of my weariness or my longing. I fear no envy, for I look for no honour or applause from a world so blind and so deceiving, which only cares for those who repay it with the most ingratitude ; and I go upon my way alone."

In many respects, however, he lost his ruggedness of disposition under the influence of Vittoria. In his last years he was glad to do justice to Bramante, against whom he had formerly made too bitter accusations. " It must be acknowledged," he wrote, " that Bramante was as great an architect as any who have appeared from ancient times to our own. It was he who laid the first foundations of St. Peter's. His clear, simple and luminous plan would not have been wrong in any single detail of that vast monument. His conception was looked upon as fine, and must be so still ; so fine, that whoever has deviated from the design of Bramante has deviated from the truth." And in his presence Vittoria could, without hurting his feelings, praise Raphael, whom he had suspected, and not without some show of reason, of having mixed in the intrigues relative to the Sixtine. " Raphael d'Urbino painted a masterpiece in Rome, which would have a just title to the first rank, if the other (the Sixtine) did not exist. It is a hall and two rooms, and the alcoves in the palace belonging to St. Peter's." Moreover, despite his grievances, he had at all times done justice to his young rival ; " and he used willingly to bestow his praise upon all," says Condivi, " even upon Raphael, though there was some rivalry between them." Bocchi relates, that after having received 500 crowns upon account for the *Sibyls* of the Pace, Raphael claimed the balance which he thought due to him, from Agostino Chigi ; the latter made some difficulty about it, and Michelangelo was called upon to arbitrate, and, filled with admiration, he replied " that each head was worth 100 crowns."

Nevertheless, his character resumed all its roughness when St. Peter's was in question. " All the nasty tricks of the San-Gallists,"[1] says Vasari, " were disgusting to the integrity of Michelangelo. One day, before he accepted the title of architect, he said openly to the foremen of the works, that

---

[1] Partisans of San Gallo.

he would advise them to combine all their efforts to keep him out of the place, for the first use that he would make of his power would be to turn them off." The cabal was for a moment upon the point of getting him dismissed. The church was said to want light. Julius III. assembled the Council. Michelangelo replied triumphantly to all the criticisms of his enemies; and then interrupting Cardinal Marcello, who was irritating him with his remarks: "I am not, and do not mean to be, compelled to tell your lordships more than any one else what I am about, and intend to do. Your business is to give me money, and to get rid of knaves; as to the building, that's my affair." Then turning to the Pope: "You see, Holy Father, what I get. If the fatigue which I endure is of no use to my soul, I am losing time and trouble." The Pope, who was fond of him, put his hands upon his shoulders and said, "You are doing much both for soul and body." At the same time Michelangelo wrote to Vasari, who was urging him to come to Florence: "If I leave Rome it would be the ruin of St. Peter's, which would be a great disgrace to me, and an unpardonable sin. When this great edifice has got to such a point that no one can possibly alter it, I hope to be able to comply with your wishes; it is, however, a mistake perhaps to make certain intriguers wait so long who are impatient for me to be gone."

Under Pius IV. the intrigues redoubled. Michelangelo was eighty-seven. His enemies declared that he was in his dotage, and was utterly ruining everything. He does seem at that time to have been discouraged for a moment, for he writes to Cardinal di Carpi: "Your lordships must have informed Messer Dandini that the construction of St. Peter's was going on as badly as possibly, which has distressed me greatly, for it is not true. Unless I am grossly deceived, I think I may declare, on the contrary, that it could not be going on better. But as it is true that my own interest and advanced age may easily impose upon me, and be injurious to this building, contrary to my intention, I intend, as soon as possible, to ask permission of his Holiness to withdraw. I likewise beg your Excellency, in order to gain time, kindly to relieve me at once of the too great responsibility which I have gratuitously undertaken for the last ten years under the commands of several Popes." He afterwards changed his mind, and a few weeks before his death retorted upon his detractors by that beautiful model of the dome, completing that of the nave, which was executed in 1546. The Greek cross of the original plan, which was changed to a Latin cross by Raphael, replaced by Baldassare Peruzzi, and again discarded by Antonio di San Gallo, was reinstated by Michelangelo.

[The architects who succeeded him carried out his plans conscientiously up to the beginning of the 17th century. But at this time, under the pontificate of Paul V., Carlo Maderno, who was commissioned to finish St. Peter's, conceived the unhappy idea of lengthening the front part of the nave, without observing that by changing the Greek into a Latin cross he diminished the effect of the dome, destroyed every feature of the edifice; and that by adding the ridiculous façade of the present building, he was taking away from a church the religious character which ought above all things to be maintained.]

However, if Michelangelo was valiantly resisting the perpetual knavery of the San-Gallists, the inevitable shadow of old age was creeping over him. One evening Julius III. requested Vasari to go and get a drawing from him. He found him alone in his workshop, working on the *Descent from the Cross* by the light of a little lantern. Talking about one thing and another, Vasari happened to cast his eyes on one of the legs of the Christ which he was intending to alter. Michelangelo dropped his lantern on purpose to prevent him seeing his work, and while he was calling Urbino to light it again, he went out of the workshop, saying, "Ah! I am so old that death is often pulling at my coat to take me away. Some day my body will fall like that lantern, and my life will go out just as it has." Another time, Vasari wrote him word that his nephew, Leonardo, had just had a son who would perpetuate the name of Buonarroti. Michelangelo replied, "My friend Giorgio, I have read your letter with much pleasure, for I see that you do not forget the poor old man. You have been at the birthday feast of a new Buonarroti. I am as much obliged as I can be for all these details; but I don't like these festivals, for man ought not to be smiling when everybody is weeping. I don't think Leonardo ought to have such rejoicing over a new-born child. This joy ought to be kept for the death of a man who has lived well."

About 1556 one of the most cruel blows fell upon him. His faithful Urbino died. He had been with him since the siege of Florence. He was more than a servant—he was a friend of every day and every moment. It was to him that he put that abrupt question one day, "What would you do if I were to die?" "I should have to find another master." "Oh! my poor Urbino! I couldn't bear you to be unfortunate:" and he gave him two thousand crowns on the spot. "He loved him so well," says Vasari, "that he waited on him in his illness, and sat up with him at night." When Vasari, who was at Florence, heard of his loss, he wrote to console him, and received this touching reply: "Messer Giorgio, my dear friend, it is hard for me to write; however, I must give you a line in answer to

Cupid   [*South Kensington*

Face page 84

Slave   [South Kensington

yours.   You know how Urbino died: it is a mark of God's great goodness, and yet a bitter grief to me.   I say a mark of God's goodness, because Urbino, after having been the stay of my life, has taught me not only how to meet death without regret, but even to long for it.   For twenty-six years I have had him with me, and have always found him perfect and faithful.   I had made him a rich man, and looked upon him as the staff and prop of my old age; and he has gone from me, leaving me nothing but the hope of seeing him again in Paradise.   I have an assurance of his happiness in the manner of his death.   He had no desire to live, but was only distressed at the thought of leaving me, laden with misfortunes, in the midst of this false and evil world.   I feel that the greater part of myself has gone with him, and all that is left me is misery and suffering.   I beg you to think of me."   About the same time he wrote to Urbino's widow, Cornelia: "No doubt you are angry with me, without being able to give me any reason for being so.   I think I understand it though, from your last letter.   When you sent me the cheeses you said that you wanted to give me something else, but that the pocket-handkerchiefs were not finished.   I replied that you were not to send me anything, so that you shouldn't spend your money upon me; but, on the contrary, that you were to ask me for something, which I should have had the greatest pleasure in giving you, for you know perfectly well what love I still have for Urbino though he is dead, and what interest I take in everything that concerns his affairs.   As to coming to you to see the children, or having little Michelangelo[1] here, I must tell you how I am situated.   It would not be advisable to send Michelangelo

---

[1] Urbino's child, and Michelangelo's godson.

G

here, because I have no womankind about me, or a suitable establishment. The child is too young and delicate yet, and some accident might happen to him, which would distress me very much. Moreover, for the last month the Duke of Florence has been making me the most eligible and tempting offers, to get me back to Florence. I have asked him for time to settle my affairs, and to be able to leave the building of St. Peter's in a satisfactory state, so that I think of staying here all the summer, and when my business is settled, and yours with the *monte-di-Pietà*, I shall come to Florence for good in the spring; for I am an old man, and shall never come back to Rome again. I shall look in upon you, and if you will give me Michelangelo I will keep him with me at Florence, and shall love him better than my nephew Leonardo's children, and will teach him what I know, and what his father would like him to learn."

Vasari kept on urging him more and more to give up the building of St. Peter's, and to join him in Florence. He answered that he was at the end of his career—"that he had not a thought which was not tinged with death;" and in his letter, among other sonnets, was the following :—

"Borne away upon a fragile bark, amid a stormy sea, I am reaching the common haven to which every man must come, to give account of the good and the evil he has done. Now I see how my soul fell into the error of making Art her idol and her sovereign lord.

"Thoughts of love, fond and sweet fancies, what will become of you, now that I am near to a double death—the one certain, the other threatening?

"Neither painting nor sculpture can avail to calm a soul which turns towards Thee, O God, who hast stretched out Thy arms upon the Cross for us."

One of his last works was for his fellow-countrymen. The Florentines wanted to resume the works of their Church San Giovanni de' Fiorentini. They asked Michelangelo, in 1559, to make them a plan for this monument. He made five. The Council of the Buildings chose the most elaborate; and when Michelangelo heard it, he said naïvely, "If they carry it out, they will have such a temple as Greece and Rome never had."

In 1562 the health of Michelangelo began visibly to decline. Vasari became anxious, and entreated Duke Cosmo to ask the Pope to have an inventory made of all Michelangelo's cartoons, models, plans, and drawings. He had already burned part of them, and they wanted to save at least all that had reference to the sacristy, façade, and library of San Lorenzo, as well as the plans which were prepared for the buildings of St. Peter's. His nephew had been told of his condition. He was to be in Rome about Lent. Michelangelo was taken with a slight fever; he saw his end approaching, and begged that Leonardo might be written to and urged to come directly; but his illness made rapid progress. In the presence of his doctor, Donati, of Daniele da Volterra, and of some others of his friends, he dictated this brief will: "I commit my soul to God, my body to the earth, and my property to my nearest relatives." He died on the 17th of February, 1563, at the age of eighty-nine, all but a few days.

Immediately after his death the Pope had his body placed in the Church of the SS. Apostoli, until a tomb should be raised for him in St. Peter's. When Leonardo arrived, the friends who had been present in Michelangelo's last moments informed him that, as he was dying, he had begged that his remains might be conveyed to Florence; but the feeling of the people of Rome had been so strong since the service which was performed at the SS. Apostoli, that they were afraid of their opposing the removal of the body; Leonardo was compelled, therefore, to enclose the body in a bale of wool, and get it out of the city by stealth.

At Florence, as soon as the arrival of the corpse was known, "All the painters, sculptors, architects," says Vasari, "assembled quietly about the Church of San Piero Maggiore. They had brought a pall of velvet, embroidered with gold, to cover the coffin and bier. At about one o'clock in the night the oldest and most distinguished among them took torches in their hands, while the younger lifted up the bier, and were proud to be the bearers of the greatest artist who had ever existed. Many persons observed this assemblage, and the whole city soon became aware that the body of Michelangelo had arrived, and was being conveyed to the Church of Santa Croce. Everything had been done, however, with the utmost secrecy, to avoid tumult and confusion. But the news passed from mouth to mouth, the church was invaded in a moment, and the academicians had great difficulty in getting as far as the chapel."

The actual obsequies were, however, deferred till the following July, so as to give time for completing the immense preparations for this national mourning. The renowned Varchi was deputed to deliver the funeral oration over Michelangelo, whose body was placed in Santa Croce, in the spot where it still rests. The monument was designed by Vasari, and executed by Battista Lorenzo.

Notwithstanding the caprices which are attributed to him, the violence of his character, his irritable and sarcastic temper, his love of solitude, which almost amounted to disease, Michelangelo was intimately associated with the most distinguished and celebrated men of his time—not reckoning the seven Popes who employed him, and with whom, despite some storms, he lived on terms of the utmost familiarity and consideration. Cardinals Pole, Bembo, Hippolytus de Medici, and so many others were among his most intimate and constant friends. As to his pupils, Sebastiano del Piombo, Daniele da Volterra, Rosso, Pontormo, Vasari, we know from the testimony of the last-named what zeal he devoted to their protection, with what generosity he gave them, not only his advice, but plans, drawings, and sometimes the entire composition of their pictures.

He seems, however, to have preferred the friendship of unimportant people, whose simple habits and ingenuousness pleased him, to that of great personages. He was attached not only to his servant Urbino, whom he treated as a friend, but to Topolino, his marble cutter, whose graceless sketches he used to correct with the utmost care, and to Menighella, "an ordinary painter of Valdarno, but a very pleasant person, who used to come from time to time and beg him to draw a St. Roch or a St. Anthony for him, from which he used to paint a picture for the country folk." Michelangelo, whom it was hard to induce to work for kings, would give up his work at once to compose simple drawings, which he adapted to the taste of his friend. Among other things, he made a model of a *Christ on the Cross* for Menighella, with a mould for making copies in cardboard, which the painter used to sell in the country; and he "used to be much amused with the little adventures which happened to the artist on the tramp."

Good and generous, loading his pupils and friends with kindness, comforting the unfortunate, giving dowries to poor girls, enriching his nephew, to whom he never gave less than three or four thousand crowns at a time,—he was himself immovable in respect to presents, "which he always looked upon as so many ties, which were irksome, and difficult to break." He used to live poorly enough, and to say à propos of this to Condivi, "Although I am rich, I have always lived like a poor man." He was hard upon himself, and even wore dog-skin gaiters upon his bare legs. He rarely admitted a friend to his table; when he was at work he was satisfied with a scrap of bread and a drop of wine, which he used to eat without breaking off from work. He lived in this frugal way up to the time when he began the last pictures in the Sixtine. Then he was an old man, and he allowed himself a simple meal at the end of the day. Michelangelo was a man of extraordinary activity, but irregular in work. He used sometimes to remain for whole months absorbed in medi- tation, without touching a brush or a chisel; then, when he had made out his composition, he would set to work with a sort of fury. He used often to give up his work in the middle, discouraged, and even in despair, because, says Vasari, " his imagination was so lofty that his hands could not express his great and awful thoughts." Generally he used to put his first idea hurriedly to paper, and afterwards take up each part in detail, or sometimes the whole, as may be seen in several of his designs, finished with the utmost minuteness. Vasari asserts that he used often to draw the same head ten or twelve times over before he was satisfied with it. Some of his studies are executed with so sure a touch that he was able to use them for models, as the bench-marks in them show; but generally he used to make little models in wax, many of which are preserved. He would attack the marble without taking precise measurements, and found himself more than once out of his calculations thereby. He took very little sleep, and used often to get up in the night to work. He used to wear a sort of cardboard helmet, which he contrived so as to hold a light, and thus the part on which he wanted to work was perfectly illuminated without any incumbrance to his hands. We possess several portraits of Michelangelo. The minute accounts which his biographers supply, and which would seem childish in the case of any other man, enable us to picture him pretty precisely. He was of middle height, with broad shoulders, slender and well proportioned; of a dry nervous temperament, his complexion was full of health and vigour, which was due as much to the regularity of his life as to nature; he had a round head, high temples, a broad square forehead with seven lines straight across it, and a nose, as is well-known, disfigured by a blow from the fist of Torrigiano; his lips were thin, the under one a little projecting, which is especially observable in the profile; his eyebrows were somewhat thick, eyes rather small than large, of the colour of horn, with scintillating specks of yellow and blue; hair black, and beard of the same colour, rather ragged, and four or five inches long, forked, and only towards the end of his life interspersed with many white hairs; his expression was agreeable, lively, and decided.

Such was Michelangelo, the last and greatest of the severe masters. This giant form closes and consummates the movement begun by Dante and Giotto, carried on by Orcagna, Brunelleschi, and Leonardo da Vinci. Though doubtless surpassed by many of his predecessors and contemporaries in some of the arts which he cultivated, this proud and gloomy genius has stamped upon his every work an awe-inspiring impress. It may be said of him that he had no ancestors; for he so immeasurably surpassed his predecessors, that notwith standing everything with which his age had endowed him, he had all the characteristics of those exceptional beings who owe to circumstances nothing but the opportunity for the free development of their extraordinary faculties. He was one of those men who derive their existence and their greatness from themselves alone, *prolem sine matre creatam;* and the day on which he finished his long and glorious career, his whole self died with him. "My knowledge," he himself said, "will give birth to a tribe of know-nothings;" and it would be unfair to hold him responsible for the extravagances of his impotent successors, who fancied that they were imitating him in their affectation of the sublime, forgetting that without force, audacity is only ridiculous. It is not alone by the creative might of his all-powerful imagination, but by an unparalleled combination of the highest and rarest faculties, that he towers above the most celebrated men of that age of prodigies. Painter, sculptor, architect, engineer, poet, citizen, he stands forth among Dante, Leonardo, Brunelleschi, Raphael, like a Titan, the last-surviving scion of a perished race, lordly commander of that army of giants. And since his character was as lofty as his genius, is not his true place the foremost among the great ones of the modern era?

APPENDIX.

CHIEFLY EXTRACTS FROM THE FAMILY ARCHIVES.[1]

THE name of Lodovico di Leonardo Buonarroti Simoni, the father of Michelangelo, is almost banished from the pages of M. Clément, and rare mention is made of his family. Michelangelo's mother, Francesca di Neri, died two years after his birth, and there is no allusion to his step-mother in any of his letters. He accustomed himself to believe that he was related to the Canossa family, and used their arms. There was, however, no relationship. Still his family was noble, though his father was content to live in poverty. He had no trade, but lived on the small income derived from his property, and showed his pride in his objection to his son's profession. While his son was in Rome, he led a life of hardship and discontent in Florence. Michelangelo's brothers would on their own account deserve little notice. Their appearance, however, is necessary in any history of him, as their behaviour is a shadow which brings out the lights in his character.

[1] For a more complete account of the family of Buonarroti, see the excellent Life of Michelangelo, recently published by Mr. C. Heath Wilson.

The eldest, Leonardo, a weakly man, became a Dominican monk. Then came Michelangelo. The third son of Lodovico was Buonarroto, whom his illustrious brother established in business. Through him the line of the Buonarroti was continued. He was in the public service in the time of Leo X., was made Count Palatine, and received various privileges from the Pope. He was Michelangelo's favourite brother and his principal correspondent.

The fourth son was Giovansimone, the scapegrace of the family, undutiful to his father, and a great trouble to his brother.

Of Sigismondo, the fifth son, little is known, save that he was a roving soldier, till he settled down and died, as a peasant, at Settignano.

The family at Florence had a hard time of it, and were selfish enough to urge Michelangelo to give up the position which he was making for himself, and come to their help. Buonarroto is sent to explain their difficulties, and especially to describe the persecutions to which Leonardo was subjected by a mercer, one Consiglio.

Michelangelo writes to his father, on the 19th August, 1497—he was twenty-two years of age, but still a minor, and under his father's control, according to Florentine law :—

Let me know what you agree to give him, and I will send it. . . . . I will try to get it together, or borrow, so that you may not have to go to the pawnbroker. . . . . Don't be surprised if I am impatient sometimes. I have much provocation from many sources. I undertook a statue for Piero de' Medici, and bought the marble, but didn't begin it because he didn't keep his word, and so I am at work upon a figure upon my own account. I bought a piece of marble for five ducats, which turned out bad, and so I lost my money. So you may see that I have to spend much and to work hard, but you shall have what you want, if I sell myself for a slave.

When Buonarroto went back, after staying with his
brother for nearly three years, he brought the good news
that Michelangelo proposed to set up Buonarroto and
Giovansimone in business at Florence.

Upon this the father writes, on the 19th December, 1500,
to say how glad he was to find that he had saved money.
He was looking out for a business for his brothers, according
to his suggestion, but had not yet met with anything to
satisfy him. He warns him against living too poorly.

> Economy is a good thing ; but, above all things, no penury. Live
> moderately, and don't do too much, and keep yourself above want,
> for the sake of your art. If you fall ill, you will be a ruined man.
> Above all things, take care of your head; keep it tolerably warm, and
> never wash yourself. Get a rub down, but no washing. Buonarroto
> tells me that you have a swelling in your side; this comes of bad
> living and over work. I have had it myself. Take care, however,
> for it is dangerous.

He ends by begging him to come to Florence—which he
did, as we know, in 1501, bringing with him a reputation
as the sculptor of the Cupid, the Bacchus, and the Pièta. It
was in August of this year that he had the commission for
the David, and in 1504 that he began his cartoon, in rivalry
with Leonardo da Vinci, for the Hall of the Signory, upon
which he was employed till early in 1505.

There is a characteristic story told by an anonymous
writer, dated 1510, which may claim a place here. Some
men of importance disputing upon a passage from Dante,
called Leonardo, who was passing, to explain it. Just then
Michelangelo also coming in sight, Leonardo said that he
would tell them what they wanted to know. Michelangelo
fancied that he was being mocked, and replied angrily,
"Explain it yourself, you who drew a horse to be made in
bronze, and gave it up because you couldn't cast it;" and

then he went away, adding, " and these Milanese blockheads believed in you."

This was the second year of the Pontificate of Julius, a period which Dr. Springer calls "the heroic age of Italian art," of which Bramante's St. Peter's, Michelangelo's paintings in the Sixtine, and Raphael's frescoes in the Stanze of the Vatican, are imperishable memorials.

M. Clément has related graphically the artist's relations with the Pope. There is, however, an interesting letter to Giuliano da San Gallo from Florence, dated the 2nd May, 1506, from which it is worth while to make some extracts.

Giuliano,—I learn from yours that the Pope is angry at my leaving, but that his Holiness is prepared both to pay me and to carry out our agreement, and that I need have no fear in coming back. As to my leaving, I heard the Pope say on Holy Saturday at table, in conversation with a jeweller and with the master of the ceremonies, that he would not spend another halfpenny either on big stones or little,— at which I was not a little surprised. However, before I left I asked for what I wanted, to carry on the work. His Holiness replied that I might come back on Monday; which I did, and again on Tuesday, Wednesday, and Thursday, as he knew; at last, on Friday, I was sent away, and the man who turned me out said that he knew who I was, but was acting under orders. . . . . There was more than this, which I will not mention. Enough that I could not help feeling that if I stayed in Rome my tomb would be built before the Pope's ; and this was the cause of my sudden departure. Now you write to me on behalf of the Pope, and so you will read this to him. Let his Holiness understand that I am more willing than ever to go on with the work. . . . .

While waiting for a reply to the above, he received another from his friend Roselli, dated Rome, May 10th, 1506, in which he related how that the Pope had sent for Bramante one evening after supper, and told him that Sangallo was going to Florence, and would bring Michelangelo back.

Bramante replied,—

Holy Father, he will not come. I know him very well, and he told me that he would not undertake the chapel . . . . and he further said, I do not believe that he is able to do it. Upon this I came forward, and, in the Pope's presence, gave Bramante the lie, and said all that I think you would have done for me. And, further, I said, " Holy Father, he never spoke to Michelangelo; and if what he has just said is true, you may cut off my head. As for him, he never spoke to Michelangelo, and I am certain he will come back when your Holiness wishes."

After the Pope had again given orders for his statue, Michelangelo sent to Florence for three assistants—Pietro Urbano, Lapo, and Lodovico. Lapo proved untrustworthy and got his dismissal, upon which Lodovico went away too. When they got to Florence they went to old Lodovico, who took their part against his son. This produced a letter from the artist, dated the 8th of February, 1507.

Dearest Father,—I have to-day received your letter, by which I see that you have been misled by Lapo and Lodovico. I hold it to be my duty to submit when you reprove me . . . . but be sure that I have done no wrong in this matter. . . . . I entreat you, therefore, not to ride the high horse when they complain of me. . .

With regard to Giovansimone, I think that he had better not come here, for the Pope is leaving this Carnival, and I think is going towards Florence. He does not leave things in order here, and the story is that there are causes for suspicion not to be inquired into or written about. Enough of this. Even if nothing happens, which I hardly expect, I will not have the burden of brothers on my shoulders. . . . I shall soon be with you, and, please God, will do all that will satisfy Giovansimone and the rest. To-morrow I will write to you about money which I mean to send you. . . . .

Meanwhile he was living in a wretched room, with a single bed in it, which he shared with his assistants. His difficulties in casting the statue were very great; but at last, when they were surmounted, he wrote to Buonarroto in November, 1807.

I had rather that you should not come back here yet, for I live in the utmost discomfort, and suffer from excessive fatigue, while I do nothing but work day and night. I have suffered, and do suffer, such fatigue that, if I had to do such another, I do not think that I should live through it. It has been a terrible work, and if another man had had it to do it would have been a bad job. I feel, however, that somebody's prayers have helped me and kept me in good health, for no one in Bologna thought that I should ever finish it after it was cast. Enough that I have carrried it through, but shall not have finished it, as I expected, by the end of this month; but next month I shall finish it and come home. . . . .

There can be no doubt that he longed to settle in his beloved city, and to be free from all his troubles in Rome. But it was not to be. He had hardly settled in Florence before the Pope called him away. Before he left, however, his father made him by law a free man. He was then thirty-three years of age. In the Florence archives, under date 28th of March, 1508, is the following entry— "Lodovico di Leonardo Buonarroti Simoni, citizen of Florence, emancipated Michelangelo his lawful son. . . ."

This, however, made no change in his relations to his family. He was still as ever ready to sacrifice himself for them.

From his letters to his father and to Buonarroto we learn much about the beginning of his work at the Sixtine. The real history of this work Dr. Springer says was this: "Soon after Michelangelo's summons to Rome, in the year 1506, the plan was settled, and Michelangelo commissioned to carry it out. His flight from Rome and residence in Bologna delayed the actual commencement until the year 1508. On the 10th of May, 1508, the master took the work in hand, but did not make much progress that year.   In the autumn of 1510 the half—the actual vault paintings—were completed.   Then followed a break of several months.   Two years later, in the autumn of 1512, shortly before All Saints' Day, the whole work was finished."

Letters to his father and brothers, in August, 1508, reveal the troubles which beset him while he was beginning these paintings.

To his father he writes :—

I have not had worse news for the last ten years than that contained in your letter. . . . . You may feel sure that all the labour I have endured has been more for you than for myself, and the property I have bought is for you while you live. If you had not been living, I should not have bought it.

If you like to let the house, or the farm, do so, and with what I can give you you will live like a gentleman.   I would say, come and live with me, were it not summer-time ; but you would not live long here in the summer.

To his brother he writes :—

Giovansimone,—They say that if you do good to a good man it makes him better, but to benefit a bad man is to make him worse. I have been trying for some years now by good words and deeds to induce you to live at peace with your father and with us, but you only get worse. . . . .

He tells him that he owes his house and living to him, and has nothing of his own ; but that he is a brute to threaten and strike his father, and that he will treat him accordingly. If he tries to do well and honour his father, he will help him as the others ; but if not, he will come to Florence and settle his affairs as he will not like.   In a postscript he says :—

I have not wandered all over Italy, and borne all sorts of mortification and hardship, torn my body with hard work, and placed my

life in a thousand dangers, except to help my family; and, now that
I have begun to raise it, you are the only one to upset and ruin in an
hour that which I have laboured so many years to do. By the body
of Christ! but you shall find that I will confound ten thousand such
as you, if needs be; therefore, be wise, and do not try a man who
has too much to bear already.

In his despondency again, at the time that he found his
first work destroyed by mould, in January, 1509, he thus
writes to his father :—

I am still in great trouble, for I have not had a penny from the
Pope for the last year, and I don't ask it, for my work does not get
on far enough to deserve payment. This is the fault of the difficulty
of the work; and then it is not my profession. So I am only losing
time without profit. God help me!

In 1512, when his work at the Sixtine was almost finished,
came the conflict between his feelings for the Medici and his
love for Florence.

On September the 15th he wrote to his father, enclosing a
short note for Giuliano de Medici.

Taxation was weighing on the Florentines.

If you are worse treated than others, refuse to pay; let them seize
what you have, and let me know. But, if you are treated in the same
way as others in the same position, be patient, and hope in God.

Live on, and if you are not to share in the honours of this world
like other citizens, it is enough to have bread, and to live in the faith
of Christ, as I do. For I live humbly; I do not care for the life or
honours of this world. I endure great weariness and hopelessness,
and so it has been with me for the last fifteen years—never an hour's
comfort. You have never known or believed how I have striven to
help you. God forgive us all! I am ready, as far as I can, to do
always the same so long as I live.

His simple words on the conclusion of his work are worth
recording.

I have finished the chapel which I painted. The Pope is very well
satisfied, but other things do not happen as I wish.

There are no letters of especial interest until the time when Michelangelo was at Carrara. There he heard from Buonarroto news of his father's illness, and in reply begs his brother to inform him of any imminent danger, and to arrange that he may want nothing needful to his soul or body, for, he says, "I have laboured only for him."

Lodovico, however, did not die, but lived to exhibit his usual weakness of mind and peculiarity of temper.

On Michelangelo's journey from Rome he visited Florence, but the old man left his house, and went off to his villa at Settignano. The son was greatly distressed and, complains in a letter upon the subject that the old man should declare that he had driven him away. Never from his birth had he wronged him. He had forgotten all that had been done for him and his sons for thirty years.

No more is wanting (he says) to fill the measure of my troubles endured for love of you. I will, however, assume that I sent you away—that I have caused you pain and annoyance, and for all these things I ask your pardon. Consider this as pardoning a son who has led a bad life, and done you all the harm possible in the world. . . . . I am anxious to go, but cannot till I have seen you at home and spoken to you. Therefore I beseech you to put away your anger and come back.

Lodovico did not die, however, till the beginning of 1534 at Settignano. His remains were brought to Florence. Michelangelo grieved over the loss of the father, to whom he had been devoted through life (but who made so unworthy a return for his generous devotion), and spared no expense in his funeral.

During the time that he was employed on the Pauline chapel, Michelangelo fell ill. The Pope and the principal

H

men made daily inquiries for him. His nephew, Leonardo, son of Buonarroto, who was dead, hastened to Rome, but was only met by his uncle's charge that he had been urged to kill him to see if he left anything. He tells him that he need not think of that, for he had made his will. Such was the bitter feeling to which the ingratitude of his family had given birth.

Still his letters are not always in this strain. During his busy years in Rome, Leonardo was his chief correspondent. They are mainly of a domestic character, referring to presents, investments, and alms. " I want to give fifty crowns for the love of God, part for the soul of Buonarroto the father, part for my own. Take care you give when there is need, and not for the sake of relationship or friendship, but for the love of God."

Occasionally there is a glimpse of his pride. "I never was a painter or sculptor to sit in a ' bottega.' I have striven for the honour of my father and brothers ; and if I have served three Popes, it has been because I was forced to do it." . . . "Some day I will tell you about our origin, where we came from, and when we settled in Florence."

To restore his family to position he made several purchases of landed property, and was not a little anxious about the perpetuation of his line through his nephew.

The year after the old man lost his most loved Vittoria Colonna, his brother Giovansimone died. He writes of him to Leonardo : "I would remind you that I grieve for the loss of a brother. You write respecting his death that he was sincerely contrite ; if so, it is enough for his son's welfare. What he has left goes to his brother 'Gismondo, for he died intestate."

He was anxious for his nephew to be settled, but would not advise him in the choice of a wife. He was to look for character, not money, for a wife who was submissive, and not always wanting to be going about to parties. " No one can say that you want to ennoble yourself by marriage, for it is well known that we are as ancient and noble citizens of Florence as any."

He bought Leonardo a house in the Ghibelline quarter of Florence, which was left to the city by the last of his descendants, in 1858. It bears the arms of Leonardo, and a bronze bust of Michelangelo over the door. It contains many works of art, manuscripts, and memorials of the artist, among them the wonderful relief which was done when he was a boy.

On the 22nd of April, 1553, he writes to his nephew :—"Leonardo, I learn from thine that the arrangement with the daughter of Donato Ridolfi has been completed. God be praised. May it be followed by His blessing." Again, on the 20th of May : "I shall show that she is the wife of my nephew."[1] In March 1554 he was anticipating the birth of his nephew's child, and bids him perpetuate the name of his father if it should be a boy, or of his mother if a girl, "either Buonarroto or Francesca." I should like to preserve this name of Buonarroto in our house, as it has lasted for three hundred years." We read his letter to Vasari when a son was born, in M. Clément's account.

It is pleasant to notice in his letters the improvement in his spirit and temper as old age comes on him. This, too, M. Clément dwells upon. He often alludes to his will. His remaining brother, Sigismund, was to divide his property

---

[1] He settled 1500 ducats upon his nephew's wife, Cassandra, and gave her two rings, one set with a diamond, the other with a ruby.

with his nephew; and, in the event of there being no heir of the family name, it was to go to "San Martino:" it was to provide for the poor, for the love of God.

One of the last letters in the Buonarroti archives shows us the old man, who was surrounded by devoted friends, and passing his life in peace, roused up by a letter from his nephew, which conveyed some false rumours circulating in Florence. "I tell you I couldn't be better or more faithfully served; and as to being robbed, I have people in my house in whom I place the utmost confidence. Look after your own affairs, not mine. I know how to take care of myself if needs be. I am not a baby."

Mr. C. D. E. Fortnum, in a pamphlet upon " The original portrait of Michelangelo by Leo Leone " (1875), says :—" No more than eight of the existing portraits of Michelangelo can be considered as authentic, and several of these on merely presumptive evidence.   1. The bronze bust of the capitol. 2. The marble bust (after Vasari, in Santa Croce, at Florence), a posthumous work.   3. Leo Leone's medal. 4. The painted portrait by Daniele, in the Trinita de' Monti fresco.   5. Marcello Venusti's portrait, in his copy of the Last Judgment.   6. The portrait ascribed to Venusti in the Casa Buonarroti.   7. The print by Bonasoni."

CHRONOLOGY, PRINCIPAL WORKS
BIBLIOGRAPHY

CHRONOLOGY OF
THE LIFE OF MICHELANGELO.

1475. Born at Caprese (March 6).

1488. Apprenticed to Ghirlandaio.

1489. Sculptured the *Head of a Faun*, now in the Uffizi.

1490. Quarrelled with Torriggiano.

1492. Sculptured the *Hercules*, now lost.

1493(?).Painted the *Virgin with the two Children and four Angels*, now in the National Gallery.

1495. Went to Bologna and Venice.

1496. Arrived at Rome (June 25).

1497. Sculptured the *Cupid*, now in the South Kensington Museum.

1498. Sculptured the *Bacchus*, now in the National Museum, Florence.

1499. Sculptured the *Pietà*, now in St. Peter's, at Rome.

1501. Received a commission to execute the *David*, in Florence.

1503. Sculptured the *Virgin and Holy Child*, now in Notre Dame at Bruges.

1504. The statue of *David*, erected in front of the Palazzo Vecchio.

—— Painted for Angelo Doni the *Holy Family*, now in Florence.

—— Commenced his cartoon for *The Battle of Pisa*.

1505. Began the *Tomb of Julius II.*, at Rome.

1507. Completed, at Bologna, the bronze statue of *Julius II.*, which was destroyed in 1511.

—— Began the *frescoes* in the Sixtine Chapel.

1509(?).Drew a cartoon of *Venus caressed by Love*, (now in the Naples Museum) from which a painting was made by Pontormo.

1512. Finished the *frescoes* in the Sixtine Chapel.

1516 to 1521. } These years were chiefly passed in the Marble Quarries, at Carrara.

1520. Commenced building the *Sacristy of San Lorenzo*, at Florence.

1527. Worked at the *Tombs of the Medici*, in San Lorenzo.

1529. Made Director of Fortifications at Florence.

—— Painted the picture of *Leda* (lost).

1531. Worked at the *Tomb of Julius II.*
—— Made design for the painting of *The Fates.*
1534. His father, Lodovico Buonarroti, died.
—— Commenced *The Last Judgment*, for the Sixtine Chapel.
1535. Appointed architect, painter, and sculptor, to the Vatican, by Paul III.
1538. Made the acquaintance of Vittoria Colonna.
1541. Finished his fresco of *The Last Judgment* (December 25).
1542. Worked at his statue of *Moses.*
—— Worked on the paintings of the Pauline Chapel.
1547. Appointed architect to St. Peter's on the death of San Gallo.
1548. Purchased the Casa Buonarroti, Florence.
1552. His appointment as architect to St. Peter's, confirmed by Julius III.
1555. Finished the *Medici Tombs*, in San Lorenzo.
—— His servant, Urbino, died.
1558. Made a model for the *Cupola* of St. Peter's.
1564. Died Feb. 18, in his eighty-ninth year, at his house in Rome.
—— Buried, in July, in Santa Croce, Florence.

POPES DURING
THE LIFE OF MICHELANGELO.
(With the dates of their election.)

A.D.
1492. Alexander VI., R. L. Borgia (*a Spaniard*).
1503. Pius III., F. T. Piccolomini.
—— Julius II., Julian della Rovere (*of Genoa*).
1513. Leo X., Giovanni de' Medici.
1522. Adrian VI. (*of Utrecht*).
1523. Clement VII., Giulio de' Medici.
1534. Paul III., Alessandro Farnese.
1550. Julius III., Giovanni Maria Giocci.
1555. Marcellus II., Cardinal Cervini.
—— Paul IV., G. P. Caraffa (*of Naples*).
1559. Pius IV., G. A. Medichini (*of Milan*).

PRINCIPAL WORKS OF MICHELANGELO STILL EXISTING.

SCULPTURE.

	Now in—
HEAD OF A FAUN, 1489. *From the antique*	National Museum, Florence
THE COMBAT OF THE GIANTS, 1490. *Bas relief*	Casa Buonarroti, Florence.
THE VIRGIN WITH THE INFANT CHRIST AND ST. JOHN, two other infants in back ground, 1490. *Bas relief*	Casa Buonarroti, Florence
ANGEL WITH CANDELABRUM. *On the tomb of San Domenico*	Bologna.
BACCHUS, 1497. *Life size statue*	National Museum, Florence.
CUPID KNEELING, 1497	S. Kensington Museum.
MADONNA DELLA PIETÀ, 1499	St. Peter's, Rome.
DYING ADONIS, 1501	National Museum, Florence.
MADONNA AND CHILD, 1503	Notre Dame, Bruges.
HEAD OF A WOMAN, 1503	S. Kensington Museum.
ST. MATTHEW, 1503	Accademia, Florence.
THE VIRGIN SEATED, holding the Infant Christ in her arms, 1503-4	Uffizi, Florence.
MEDALLION—the Virgin and Child and St. John, 1503-4	Royal Academy, London.
DAVID, 1504. *Colossal statue*	Accademia, Florence.
TOMB OF POPE JULIUS II., 1505 to 1542	San Pietro in Vincoli, Rome.
THE CAPTIVES—chained, 1505. *Two statues*	Louvre, Paris.
MOSES, 1513 to 1520. *Colossal statue*	San Pietro in Vincoli, Rome.
TOMB OF GIULIANO DE' MEDICI, 1520 to 1534	San Lorenzo, Florence.
TOMB OF LORENZO DE' MEDICI, 1520 to 1534	San Lorenzo, Florence.

BRUTUS, 1529 ? *A bust* .   .   . National Museum, Florence.
CHRIST TAKEN DOWN FROM THE CROSS.
   Colossal statue. Finished by Federigo
   Frizzi   .   .   .   .   .   . S. Maria del Fiore, Florence
MADONNA AND CHILD .   .   .   . San Lorenzo, Florence
THE DEAD CHRIST, THE TWO MARIES,
   AND JOSEPH OF ABIMATHEA   .   . San Lorenzo, Florence.

PAINTINGS.

THE VIRGIN, INFANT CHRIST, ST. JOHN
   AND ANGELS, 1493-95 ? .   .   . Stoke Park.
THE HOLY FAMILY, 1504   .   .   . Uffizi, Florence.
ENTOMBMENT OF OUR LORD. *Unfinished* National Gallery, London.
MADONNA AND HOLY CHILD AND ST.
   JOHN. *Unfinished* .   .   .   . National Gallery, London.
THE PARCÆ, 1531-32. *The composition*
   is by Michelangelo : but the painting
   is thought to be by Rosso .   .   . Pitti Palace, Florence.
FRESCOES ON THE CEILING, 1507 to 1512 Sixtine Chapel.
THE LAST JUDGMENT. *Finished* 1541. Sixtine Chapel.
THE CONVERSION OF ST. PAUL ; and
   THE CRUCIFIXION OF ST. PETER.
   Finished in 1519 .   .   .   . Pauline Chapel.

BIBLIOGRAPHY

1893. J. A. SYMONDS. Michaelangelo Buonarotti.

1904. A. CONDIVI. Life of Michel Angelo.

1906. E. BOROUGH JOHNSON. Michael Angelo. Drawings of Great Masters Series.

1906. G. GRONAU. Michael Angelo.

1911. SIR. CHAS. HOLROYD. Michael Angelo Buonarotti. With translation of the life of the master by his scholar, A. Condivi.

1912. ROMAIN ROLLAND. Michael Angelo.

1913. R. W. CARDEN (Editor). Record of Life as told in his own letters and papers.

1921. GEORG. M. C. BRANDES. Michelangelo Buonarotti.

1924. E. V. LUCAS. Michel Angelo. (Little Books on Great Masters Series).

1924. GERALD S. DAVIES. Michelangelo. (Classics of Art Series).

1927. O. E. OLLIVIER. Michelangelo.

1928. A. VENTURI. Michelangelo.

INDEX

INDEX.

The GREAT ARTISTS

Studies of the Lives and Works of the Great Artists of the English, Italian, French, Spanish and Dutch Schools

WRITTEN BY EMINENT CRITICS

Each volume illustrated with Eight Plates in half tone

EDITED WITH FOREWORD BY HORACE SHIPP AND FLORA KENDRICK SHIPP, A.R.B.S.

Crown 8vo. Cloth. Price 2/6 net per volume

SAMPSON LOW, MARSTON & CO., LTD.

The Plan of the Series

✢✢

OF books upon art and artists there is no end, every publishing season bringing from the press its own vast contribution. Amid the consequent embarrassing wealth of information and idea the student of art—whether an actual student at a school or a lover of art searching information—may easily find his or her elementary needs unsupplied. Those needs as we have seen them, are before all else a knowledge of the artist's life and environment looked at alongside the record of actual achievement in works of art. With these facts before us, an indication where the originals may be found, enough in the way of reproduction to convey something of the characteristics of the painter, and a minimum of theorising, the foundations may well be laid upon which judgment and personal preferences can be built.

This has been the aim of the Great Artist Series. Written by the most eminent critics of the last generation, they endeavour to state the facts so that the man and his work can speak thereafter. In most instances few fresh facts have come to light since the books were written; so that the modern method of writing upon art which is much more subjective, more the critic and less the artist, more theory and less fact, may safely be added to this preliminary knowledge. To this end each volume will contain a bibliography of the important English works to be consulted. As these books have been chosen from English sources because the obvious next step in study is the reading of books in our own language, so the illustrations have, as far as possible, been chosen from English Galleries that students may consult the originals, and yet have reproductions at hand for reference.

By thus definitely limiting the scope of the series to first needs and basic facts it is hoped that they will serve the purpose for which they were designed—to bring authoritatively before the reader the lives and works of the great artists.

SELF PORTRAIT

English Painters

ENGLISH painting begins much later than that of the continental
countries, but its glories stand self-confessed in every gallery.
The great portrait masters of the 18th century : Reynolds,
Gainsborough, Romney and Lawrence ; the landscape painters,
Constable and Turner ; the water-colourists, Cox and Peter de Wint ;
the genre picture painters, Sir David Wilkie and Mulready ; Hogarth
and Cruikshank, literary masters of the brush and graver and both
creators of types ; and the animal painter, Sir Edwin Landseer, whose
work is emerging again now from a period of neglect.

The ten volumes which cover the painters' lives give a fairly complete
picture of the last two centuries in England. From the urbane days
of the eighteenth century whereof we see the high society through the
eyes and lives of the fashionable portrait painters, we pass down to the
life of the 19th century in the drawings of a Wilkie, a Mulready, or a

3

Cruikshank. Greatest of all presenters of the life of his times Hogarth shows us his period with the satirist's brush and graver.

Alongside this pageant of men and women we have the English landscape. We have so many of Turner's pictures in our own galleries that his reputation has never received that international support which it deserves. The English water-colourists, on the other hand, have been universally acclaimed, and no single school of painters has brought such honour to this difficult medium.

In these ten books: Reynolds by F. S. Pulling; Lawrence and Romney by Lord Ronald Gower; Gainsborough and Constable by G. Brock-Arnold; Turner by Cosmo Monkhouse; Wilkie by J. W. Mollett; Hogarth by Austin Dobson; Mulready by F. G. Stephens who also writes the volumes on Cruikshank and on Landseer; and David Cox and de Wint by G. R. Redgrave, we have an epitome of English painting and English life and landscape which will bring the many fine works in our great collections into living relationship with their times and their creators.

Italian Painters and Sculptors

AT times one is tempted to think that the study of art coincides with the study of that art which came into being with the rise of humanism during the Italian Renaissance. From the days when painting and sculpture emancipated themselves from Byzantine influence under Cimabue and his great pupil Giotto, or in the hands of the Pisans, through the excellences of the various schools to the autumn glory of the Renaissance at Venice with Titian and Tintoretto, the art centre of the world was Italy.

The lives of the artists and their relationships with one another and with their powerful patrons make reading as fascinating and as coloured as their great pictures. Many of them were not only master painters but great men of action, courtiers, friends of popes and princes. Their lives and their works were inextricably united to give expression to those full-flavoured days.

The twelve volumes in this series takes us through this magnificent period of Italian life and art. From Giotto and Fra Angelico, the painters of the 13th and 14th centuries; to Mantegna, Francia and Correggio, respective figures of the Paduan, Umbrian and Lombardy schools in the 15th and early 16th centuries; thus to the Florentines, Bartolommeo and Albertini and the later del Sarto; finally to Titian and Tintoretti in the great days of Venice. Three figures, out-topping all others even in this period, demand special attention: Leonardo da Vinci, Raphael and Michelangelo.

4

MADONNA OF THE ROCKS

So the Renaissance lies spread before us in a series of studies of the lives and works of the artists : Giotto by Harry Quilter ; Fra Angelico and the early Florentine painters by C. M. Phillimore ; Mantegna and Francia in one volume by Julia Cartwright ; Corregio by M. Compton Heaton ; the three Florentines, Bartolommeo, Albertini and Andrea del Sarto dealt with by Leader Scott in one volume ; the same author treats the sculptors in two volumes, one upon Ghiberti and Donatello and the earliest sculptors, and the other, Della Robbia, Cellini and the later sculptors ; Titian by R. F. Heath ; Tintoretto by W. R. Ostler ; Leonardo by Dr. J. Paul Richter ; Michelangelo by Charles Clement ; and finally Raphael by N. D'Anvers.

5

THE BENT TREE

French and Spanish Painters

TO the modern student of art Paris is the centre of a world of warring schools since the Impressionists took painting away from the representation of objective nature to the presentation of individual idea. Earlier periods of French art, however, have yielded great names: Claude de Lorrain, one of the fathers of landscape ; Watteau, the exponent of French grace ; the landscape painters of Barbizon, Corot, Daubigny and Dupré, and Millet, Rousseau and Diaz ; these with the nineteenth century painters of subject pictures, Vernet, Delaroche and Meissonier, carry us to the reactions towards impressionism.

In our series O. J. Dullea writes on Lorrain ; J. W. Mollett has a volume upon Watteau among early painters, and one upon Meissonier ; the painters of Barbizon are dealt with in two volumes by J. W. Mollett ; and Vernet and Delaroche are treated in one volume by J. Ruutz Rees.

Two volumes are devoted to two great Spanish Masters: Velasquez by E. Stowe, and Murillo by Ellen E. Minor.

German, Flemish and Dutch Painters

IF the Latin countries have given us the classic conceptions both in religious figure painting and in landscape, painting became human as its vortex moved to the North. Even the earliest German masters with their Gothic Madonnas and Christs had a breathing humanity to pit against the increasing intellectualism of the South. With the advent of Dürer we are in a world of humans. But it was with the Flemish and Dutch painters at the beginning of the 17th century that this Northern art found its full blossoming, with Rembrandt and Rubens, with Franz Hals and Van Dyck and the lovely figure and interior painters of Holland. The art of these Teutonic countries is covered in the series in eight volumes: Dürer by R. F. Heath; the Little Masters of Germany by W. B. Scott; Holbein, greatest of all portrait painters surely, by Joseph Cundall; Rubens by C. W. Kett; Vandyck and Hals in one volume by P. R. Head; the Figure Painters of Holland by Lord Ronald Gower and the Landscape Painters by Frank Cundall; last, and perhaps greatest of all, Rembrandt by J. W. Mollett.

A Series of Illustrated Biographies of

THE GREAT ARTISTS

Price **2/6** net.
PER VOL.

Re-edited by

HORACE SHIPP and FLORA KENDRICK, A.R.B.S.

Lightning Source UK Ltd.
Milton Keynes UK
UKOW021948130313

207604UK00007B/46/P